the
Great
Lakes

St. Lawrence R.

1669

1679

Lake Ontario

1540

Lake Erie

1812

1776

1778

Atlantic Ocean

OPEN DOOR
TO THE
GREAT LAKES

OPEN DOOR TO

Written and illustrated by DIRK GRINGHUIS

THE GREAT LAKES

DUELL, SLOAN and PEARCE NEW YORK

| DUELL, SLOAN & PEARCE AFFILIATE OF MEREDITH PRESS | *Library of Congress Catalog Card Number: 66-17032* |

Manufactured in the United States of America for Meredith Press

For CHARLES RUFFING

who made OPEN DOOR possible

The author wishes to thank the following staff members of The Museum, Michigan State University, for their help in editing the manuscript:

Dr. Rollin H. Baker, Director of the Museum, Professor of Zoology and Fisheries and Wildlife;

Charles L. Cleland, Acting Head, Department of Archaeology;

Leslie C. Drew, Curator of Exhibits, Instructor in Natural Science.

CONTENTS

IMPORTANT DATES IN THE
HISTORY OF THE GREAT LAKES

13,000 B.C.: Early man crosses the Bering Straits.

10,000 B.C.: The time of the last glacier.

1000 A.D.: Viking explorers sail to our shores.

1535: Jacques Cartier claims Canada for the French.

1615: Champlain explores Georgian Bay and Lake Huron.

1622: Brulé reaches Lake Superior.

1634: Nicolet discovers Lake Michigan.

1641: The first mission is built at Sault Ste. Marie.

1669: Lake Erie is discovered by the French.

1673: Father Marquette and Joliet travel down the Mississippi to the mouth of the Arkansas.

1679: The first sailing ship on the Lakes, the *Griffin*, is launched and lost.

1701: Fort Pontchartrain is built by the French at Detroit.

1715: Fort Michilimackinac is built at the Straits.

1754: Beginning of the French and Indian War.

1763: The war is over, and Canada is given to England. Pontiac begins his rebellion.

1764: British retake their frontier forts.

1777: Indians and British raid settlers during the Revolutionary War.

1783: End of American Revolution; boundaries are set between Canada and the new United States.

1787: Northwest Territory is formed, including the area of Ohio, Indiana, Illinois, Michigan, Wisconsin, and part of Minnesota.

1812: Outbreak of war with England.

1813: Oliver Hazard Perry defeats the British fleet on Lake Erie.

1814: The war is ended.

1816: The Erie Canal is begun.

1818: *Walk-in-the-Water* is launched on Lake Erie.

1829: The Welland Canal bypasses Niagara Falls.

1853: The Sault Canal and locks are begun.

1855: The Sault Canal and locks are opened.

1871: The great fire levels the city of Chicago.

1957: Big Mac, the Mackinac Bridge across the Straits, is opened.

1959: The St. Lawrence Seaway is completed, linking the Great Lakes with the Atlantic Ocean.

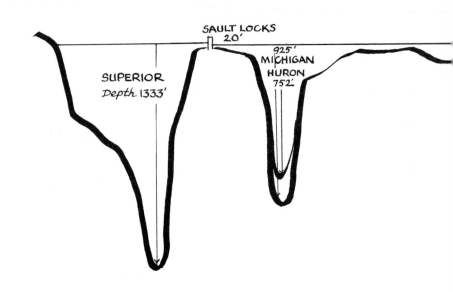

SAULT LOCKS
20'

SUPERIOR
Depth 1333'

925'
MICHIGAN
HURON
752'

THE ICE GIANT

High in the great ice fields of the north a snowflake fell. Others followed, whirled in by the fierce storms that howled about the valley shaped like a half-moon. The snow grew deeper. Avalanches formed and crashed down inside the steep walls. The snow grew heavy. Because of the great pressure, water began trickling down and freezing at the base. At last, the entire basin, or "cirque," was one immense mass of ice. The ice giant was born. Too large for his cradle, he started forward. The first great glacier had begun its journey.

This all began in the Hudson's Bay–Labrador region. The time was around one million years ago.

And now the land waited . . . a land of valleys and trees

and hills and ancient rivers . . . and animals, strange monstrous creatures some of them, unaware of what was coming down from the north to change the land and their lives once again, as it had been changed many times in the past.

Slowly the ice cap moved . . . a few feet at a time, retreating, moving on again . . . a glacier over nine thousand feet thick in places! Carefully it thrust powerful fingers into old river beds, dug, widened, flattened. As it moved it picked up debris, rock and dirt called *glacial till*. Some it spread in thin layers; some in huge piles. Bumping, grinding, grooving, polishing, it kept on. Some of the glacial till was left at the ice cap's edge, forming *marginal moraines*. Other debris was carried the full length of the journey. And finally the ice giant covered four million square miles of North America. Now it reached from Hudson's Bay clear down to central Illinois, Indiana, and Ohio. Then, as the climate grew warm, it stopped at the Ohio River. Melting, it began to retreat.

At its stopping place it left a long ridge called a *terminal moraine*. At its edges were the marginal moraines. Ancient river valleys had become basins. Rivers, filled with debris, sent their waters into the basins. The ancestors of our present Great Lakes were started.

But it still wasn't over. The glacier retreated, advanced, retreated again. Five times the mighty ice cap moved, scooping the old basins even deeper, joining smaller basins together into one huge bowl.

Finally, about twelve thousand years ago, the last of the ice caps, called the Wisconsin glacier, retreated. Now, relieved of the crushing weight of ice, the earth's surface began to rise, to spring back. As the huge sheet of water left by the melting ice receded, the land appeared once more.

It was a changed land. Rivers now flowed in different directions, cutting gorges, making waterfalls. And then, as

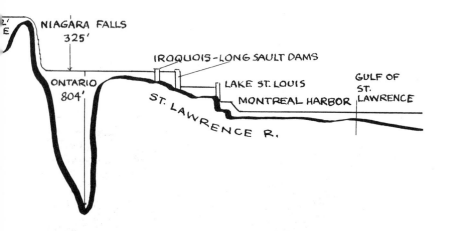

NIAGARA FALLS
325'

IROQUOIS-LONG SAULT DAMS

ONTARIO
804'

LAKE ST. LOUIS

GULF OF
ST.
LAWRENCE

MONTREAL HARBOR

ST. LAWRENCE R.

OPEN DOOR
TO THE
GREAT LAKES

though glad to be free, the earth took a deep breath. The land tilted, our Great Lakes were formed. One section to the west rose higher than the others, dropping Lake Ontario over three hundred feet below Lake Erie.

As for the glacial till, it remained. It was only a few inches deep in some areas, a thousand feet deep in others. Long narrow ridges called *eskers* were left where the debris had been gently deposited. Tall round hills called *kames* told of where the water had flowed into funnel-shaped ice cracks.

Rivers now followed the new hills, changing course and even direction. Some ancient river channels filled with still water and returning vegetation. These became muck lands. With the lowering water level, westerly winds tossed and heaped quartz crystals into ridges and hills called sand dunes.

The rise and fall of the land masses had been like a seesaw. Land forms balanced themselves as weight on one section of the land and caused upheavals on the opposite section. Finally, with the rebound of the land, our present system of lake outlets came into being. As the lake levels dropped, the water no longer flowed through the Chicago outlet into the Illinois River. Instead Lakes Superior, Michigan, and Huron now flowed through the St. Clair River into Lake Erie, over the falls at Niagara into Lake Ontario, and on to the sea.

These are the Great Lakes as we know them today. They are bordered by eight states: Minnesota, Wisconsin, Illinois, Michigan, Ohio, Indiana, Pennsylvania, New York, and the Canadian Province of Ontario. The largest collective body of fresh water in the world, these lakes cover 95,000 square miles.

As for the glacier that formed them, how do we know it really existed? At one time it was thought that a great flood had come down from the north washing gravel, sand, clay, and rock southward. Large boulders were thought to have been carried by floating icebergs. From this idea came the word *drift,* a term meaning all debris that is carried by a glacier.

Today, geologists have a great deal of information about the glaciers themselves. And while there are no glaciers within hundreds of miles of our Great Lakes today, there are still glaciers to be studied.

Two types of glaciers are available to the geologist. There are mountain glaciers, such as those in the Alps of Europe or the tall Himalayas of Asia. There are also mountain glaciers high in the peaks above tropical Mexico, where the snow never melts. In our own nation, southern Alaska has hundreds of these mountain glaciers.

As for the great continental glaciers, there are only two. One nearly covers Greenland; the other covers the continent of Antarctica.

By examining these existing ice caps, it was found that the glacial deposits were the same as those forming the soils of the Great Lakes area. And the mixture of rock materials there—ranging in size from boulders to bits of clay, called glacial till—is also found across the Great Lakes region.

Another clue lies in the different rocks scattered over wide areas, far from their source. Copper and iron, for example, a product of Michigan's Upper Peninsula, have been found far to the south. From Canada have come bits and pieces of jasper conglomerate, a rock peculiar to that area but which can be found scattered along the trail of the ice giant.

There is a difference in soils also in areas that escaped the ice cap. These regions have soil made from the weathering and breaking down of bedrock. Often, the ancient bedrock itself is covered with its own soil. But in the glacier regions, the ancient bedrock is covered instead with glacial drift, sometimes to a depth of twelve hundred feet. And so the soils of the Great Lakes region are young and very mixed.

Further evidence is found in the land shapes. One of the easiest to trace is in the hills or moraines that may run for many miles across the country. In back of these hills where the ice retreated, there is usually a band of low earth formations, showing the sag and swell of the earth. In front of the moraine a flat expanse tells of the running off of melting water.

Even clearer for the geologist's study are the carvings, scoring, and polishing of exposed rocks—rocks which still carry the scars of the giant's passing.

As for the million years that have passed since the Ice Age began, they are only a clock tick in the thousands of millions of years of the earth's history.

Once again, science helps the story to unfold. Geology, the science of earth history, studies the rocks, plants, animals, and minerals that make up our world. The records are found in the rocks—museums of the past resulting from the shaping and reshaping of the earth over very long periods of time.

On the surface, rocks are constantly affected by moisture and air. Plant roots and frost also split them apart, while some types are washed away by water. Rock pieces, loosened by this weathering, often roll down mountains and form piles of slide-rock. Heavy rains cause landslides. Bits of rock are then picked up and carried to the sea by rivers. Swift streams may even carry boulders, pushing and bumping them along until they take on a rounded form.

All of these actions wear down the surface of the earth. But at the same time, powerful forces inside the earth cause new mountains to rise or rock layers to wrinkle. Sometimes rock inside the earth gives way beneath the great strain and slip. This is called a *fault*. When this takes place, the jar that is felt is called an earthquake.

Geologists today believe that the earth is many millions of years old. Recent proof has been added through the use of a test called the carbon-14 Test. This process tests the amount of carbon present in organisms. And because all living things build carbon during life and lose it at a known rate after death, C-14 tests detect the amount of carbon still present. They can, therefore, very closely tell the age of the object. C-14 tests, however, can go back only thirty thousand years. More recent tests make it possible to predate matter over a far longer span. Tests for potassium argon in volcanic rock, for example, have shown that man the toolmaker goes back to 1,750,000 years instead of one million years as previously thought.

The age of the earth is divided into eras and periods. Each era is like a separate book in which the earth's long story is divided into periods.

The beginning of life is called the Archeozoic Era, recent life the Cenozoic Era.

No one knows exactly how life began on earth. Most scientists believe that it started first in the shallow seas. And because animals depend on plants for food, the first life was probably plant life.

Rocks formed in this first life era are, of course, the oldest known. They also lie the deepest. One of the most common forms is granite, a rock which contains no sign of life forms. Near the close of this earliest period, dim traces begin to appear of very small creatures and plants. Next, a great upheaval on the earth's crust raised up the Laurentian Mountains in Canada, then leveled out to form a low plain in North America. In the seas, animals and plants were growing larger.

Next came the age of primitive life, the Paleozoic Era. Now large parts of our continent were covered with shallow seas. These seas wore away the hills, carrying the material across the land, letting it settle to the bottom. This material, called sediment, formed new rocks called *sedimentary*.

These rocks were formed in wide areas around the Great Lakes, some of them ten miles thick. While these rocks were forming, important minerals, such as iron ore, came into being.

At the end of this era, molten rock or lava came pouring up out of the cracks in the earth's surface. With the lava came nickel, copper, silver, and gold.

With the next age, the Mesozoic Era, the story of life becomes clearer. For in the rocks were pictured the swarming life of this ancient time. The pictures were of fossils.

Fossils are of three types: the preserved remains of the actual body of the plant or animal; molds left after the actual body disappeared; and footprints or trails.

In this first age of the creatures without backbones, called *invertebrates*, there were no flowering plants or land animals. But thousands of fossils, such as *trilobites*, have been collected from the rocks. Trilobites were crab-like animals with three body sections. Related to the crab, shrimp, and lobster, they have now disappeared from the seas. *Crinoids*, plantlike animals, still exist in similar form in some warm ocean waters. Others also left their record. For the seas were heavy with lime, and the shelled animals increased. When they died, they left their hard shells behind.

As for the seas themselves, they left immense amounts of limestone as well as other important rocks, such as slate and marble. Petroleum and natural gas were formed in these ancient rock beds.

With the next period, life underwent further change.

Strange fishes swam in the waters, scorpions and thousand-legs crept up onto the land and became the first animals to breathe air. Green plants flourished, but there were no trees or flowers.

Then, in the next period, thick sediments were laid down by the retreating waters in New York and Pennsylvania. Forests began to appear, and in the seas were fishes with backbones, while on the land crawled the first air-breathing fishes, the amphibians.

Finally, nearly all of North America was dry land. After a time, thick growths of ferns, rushes, and trees sprang up in the swamps. As they died and fell back into the water, they were covered by other dead plants. The weight of these layers buried beneath the sediment finally squeezed out the water. Lignite was formed and finally coal. The climate was hot, tropical.

Slowly the climate changed until it was cold. Now even greater changes took place on the land. Above the splashing amphibians, insects buzzed. And then came the reign of the terrible reptiles, the mighty dinosaurs.

But this era, one of the most fascinating of all, must remain a blank in our Great Lakes area. For with the coming of the glaciers, all trace of the mighty monsters was scoured away.

With the end of the dinosaurs, the Cenozoic Era began, the time of recent life in which our world is still living. Now the continents took on their present shapes. There were trees, brightly colored birds, wily mammals, reptiles, insects. Some died or retreated before the pushing glaciers; some returned. Across the continent were forms we know today, the Grand Canyon, the Great Plains, and the Great Lakes themselves.

The weathering and the aging process still continue. The uppermost rocks laid down are still new and have not yet hardened. Even Niagara Falls is gradually reshaping the rocks over which it tumbles. The water flows from Lake Erie to Lake Ontario, becoming a foaming cataract that erodes the cliff year after year. Now it has worked backward, forming a three-hundred-foot gorge running seven miles back to the falls themselves.

Will there ever be another glacier? Perhaps. If so, the major seaports of the world will all be under water. But to find out, we will have to wait a few thousand years.

2

SOME ANIMAL
ANCESTORS

As the ice melted back, the trees slowly returned to a freshly scoured land. With them came the animals who had survived in the warmer southern climate.

Black and white spruce moved north first, marching over moraine and rock, then the fir, the larch, and finally the tall pine. Next came the aspen and hemlock. In the glacial valleys sugar maples began putting out leaves, green in summer, scarlet in autumn. On the plains the wiry grasses and sedges grew brilliant with the blooms of asters and goldenrod. There were shrubs as well, thousands of them.

Into this new world moved the animals and among them the mammals. Some are still here, others have either disappeared or moved on.

Mammals are animals whose young are fed from the milk of the mother. Born fully formed, they are warm-blooded, have hair or fur, a four-chambered heart and a diaphragm to aid in breathing. Except for whales and dolphins, most live on land. Some, such as the flying squirrel, can glide through the air, but only the bat can fly. Ground squirrels, moles burrow in the ground while squirrels live in trees. Some spend much of their time in the water—the beaver, otter, muskrat. Some are hoofed, such as the deer or bison. Some are carnivores—meat eaters—such as the puma or wolf.

Unlike the cold-blooded creatures before them, they now had built-in temperature controls. Cold meant slowing down for the reptiles; for the mammals it meant adapting, or adjusting to outside temperature changes. Fur grew thicker, fat layers heavier in the cold seasons. To maintain a constant body temperature, food—in varying amounts according to the size of the animal—was essential.

This adapting process was a slow and gradual one lasting over millions of years. It is still going on today. Land areas change, forests, grasslands, water, climate—all continue to vary. With these changes come changes in the animal world. Only those who can adapt to this change survive. Others die out or move on. It is the surroundings or environment that decides the survivors. Some of this adapting process is built in; other means of survival are learned. For example, if an animal is small, the approach of a hawk means danger. To the leader of a deer herd the distant howl of a wolf means it is time to keep the herd close together and be prepared to defend the fawns. At the same time, the fawns, watching the behavior of the grown-ups, learn to detect danger signals and to protect themselves. This learning is passed on to new generations by example, setting a pattern of survival.

At the end of the last Ice Age, there were animals of many

types in the Great Lakes area, each following its own pattern of behavior. Some of these patterns, such as that of the bison, nearly brought about their destruction. For others, such as the mastodons, their time simply ran out. The larger the animal, the less its chances for survival. Larger species needed more food, wider ranges. Small animals in a forest habitat found it much easier to survive.

Among the mammals, the mighty mammoth and mastodon were the largest ever to live in the land of the Great Lakes. The mammoth was covered with long shaggy hair; his tusks were giant sickles of ivory sweeping up and out. The mastodon, ancient ancestor of the elephant, had coarse hair as well but his tusks were smaller and curved only slightly.

Apparently the mammoths preferred the uplands. When they died, their skeletons were often destroyed by weather. The mastodons, however, lived in the lowlands. As they died, their skeletons were often preserved in the peat moss or marl covering their bones. Many of their remains have been found, a record of the great beasts that roamed the Great Lakes area six thousand years ago.

In this strange world of the mammoth and mastodon, there were also whales. Their remains have been found in what was once the Lake Huron basin.

Where did this great Noah's ark of animals come from? Scientists who specialize in ancient life forms, *Paleontologists*, believe that some mammals of North America arrived in a great migration about one million years ago. Most came across the land bridge that spanned the Bering Straits at that period. Some crossed and recrossed the bridge many times. Among the arrivals were the shrews, bears, weasellike mammals, wild dogs, cats, squirrels, beaver, deer, bison, mice, rabbits. With the raising of still another land bridge, the Isthmus of Panama, some mammals moved south into the forests of South America. Others, the porcupine and opossum, for example, traveled up into North America from South America.

Then with the coming of the great glaciers, many were forced to retreat south; many died. Some survived to return once more.

One shaggy beast living in the Great Lakes area after the glacier was the musk ox. Instead of dying out like the mammoth, the musk ox kept traveling north until he reached the frozen tundra of the Arctic, where he lives today. Standing about five feet at the shoulder, he gives off a strange odor of musk from which he gets his name. On his head are thick heavy horns curving down and then out into points. The brownish yellow hair on his shoulders is so heavy that he seems to be humped.

Another survivor was the mighty bison, both ancient and recent types, misnamed buffalo. At one time bision herds numbered over sixty million! Their range was from the Pacific to the Atlantic, from the Great Slave Lake south to the Gulf of Mexico.

In spite of their great size, they were quick and fast, and they swam wide rivers with ease. Congregating in huge herds, they divided into bands moving in single file to their watering places. Because of their immense strength and size as well as their herding instincts, there were few animals who dared attack them. Therefore the fighting instinct for survival was never fully developed, and they remained fairly harmless. With the coming of man, the bison were easy victims of his weapons. Finally, what was left of them moved out onto the Great Plains.

Other herds moved across the Great Lakes as well. Among them were the hoofed caribou. These wanderers, male and female, carried great hand-shaped, or *palmate*, antlers on their heads. Their wide feet made it possible for them to travel over deep snow with ease. With the coming of man, these animals, like the musk oxen, moved northward where they live today.

One of the strangest animals ever to pace a rocky ledge or glide over a pine-needled forest floor was the puma. Also known as mountain lion, cougar, or panther, he had the greatest range of any land animal. Early times found him in Alaska as well as deep at the tip of South America.

The puma is one of the handsomest members of the cat family. Quick and powerful, these carnivores are capable of great bursts of speed. In pursuing their natural prey, the deer, they can leap thirty feet in a single bound!

Moving south from the Great Lakes, pumas grew numerous in the area between the Allegheny Mountains and the Mississippi River, where there were plenty of deer and wild turkeys as well. Today, those that are left cling to the mountains of the west and northwest.

An ancestor still with us and of great importance to early man is the white-tailed, or Virginia, deer. Although they are familiar to almost everyone, they are still most unusual animals.

First, consider their antlers. These bony projections on the head are grown and shed by the males each year. Elk and moose, also members of the deer family, shed their antlers, too.

Antlers are not horns. Horns, such as those worn by cattle, goats, antelope, are hollow. When broken off they cannot grow back. But the pronged racks of the deer family are the result of a single summer's growth.

These antlers serve mostly for fighting other bucks for the possession of the does. For this reason antlers are unneeded after the mating season. Sometimes combat ends in tragedy for both. When the antlers become locked together, the animals starve. But antlers or no, deer are not the shy, harmless creatures they appear to be. Actually, when aroused, they can be as dangerous as a grizzly bear. For their razor-sharp hooves can cut an attacker into ribbons.

Season brings color changes as well as antler changes in the deer. Reddish-brown in summer, their coats turn grayish and rough in winter. But regardless of the season, the white patch on the underside of the tail remains. When running, the tail is held high like a white flag. Thus the name —white-tailed deer.

During spring, summer, and fall, the white-tails roam the countryside eating herbs and other material, such as twigs and leaves. Winter brings hardship. Without the widespread feet of the caribou, they cannot move through deep snow and are forced to herd up in dense swamps or woods called deer "yards."

Young are born usually in the spring. Twins are common. Fawns are spotted at birth and keep their spots for several months.

If the woods of the Great Lakes have a clown, honors should go to the black bear. Born furless and blind, cubs are smaller at birth than a puppy. Because they develop slowly, the mother is extremely protective of her young. Any threat brings instant and fearless attack.

When full grown, black bears are massive animals with big bare-palmed feet bearing heavy claws. Males are much larger than females. Both have teeth shaped something like a dog's with the addition of grinding molars at the back. Their hair is coarse, their tails short. And their habit of standing on their hind legs to feed or look around has made them a favorite subject for storytellers. For they have a clumsy manlike look, and they like to clown. Cubs, for example, will rear up and box with one another, growling, yapping, like two small boys fighting.

Big, strong, brave, full-grown bears seem to detest exercise. Although they are perfectly able to prey on deer, elk, or even moose, they prefer an easier way of life. So, most of their diet is made up of small mammals, insects, fish, fruits, roots, bark, berries, and nuts.

During the summer a black bear spends much of his time tearing rotten logs or stumps apart in search of fat grubs, ants, or bees. And if the bees have honey, bruin is really happy. He will go to almost any length to get the sweet stuff, even though the furious bees are swarming over his head and body, stinging him until he rolls in roaring pain on the ground. Filled at last, he will stumble off to safety, where he can lazily lick the last remaining honey and then take a nap.

By fall, bears are very fat and very lazy. It is then that they turn in for a winter's sleep.

Hibernation habits vary—if bears actually hibernate at all. Many experts feel that they go to sleep not because it is cold and snowing but because they are just too full to eat any more. Their stomachs shrink, and they begin the winter's sleep. Cubs are born at this time in the den, which may be a hollow tree, a cave, or even a dense thicket.

If the bear is the clown, the beaver is the builder. Perhaps no other animal has helped write the history of the Great Lakes more than he.

Today's beavers are descended from the giant beaver of prehistoric times and are fascinating animals to watch. A rodent, or gnawer, the beaver is related to the squirrel, mouse, and porcupine. He is also the largest rodent in North America, weighing from forty to seventy pounds. Some have even been known to reach one hundred pounds.

One of his most outstanding features are his four strong

orange-colored teeth. Two above and two below, they continue to grow throughout his lifetime, so that the cutting edges are constantly replaced. His lips can close behind these teeth making it possible for him to gnaw while under water.

Another distinctive trademark is his curious flat tail. It is from ten to twelve inches long and is an amazing and useful instrument. Shaped like a paddle blade, it is covered with horny scales and is used as a rudder when swimming. Stretched flat, it supports him when sitting upright. Under water it becomes a sort of propeller. It is also an alarm. Should a hawk or other predator threaten, the beaver will smack the water with his flat tail. This signal means "dive" to young and old alike.

The strong webs between the five long toes permit the hind feet to help in swimming. The beaver is a swift swimmer, whereas he is clumsy on land; his forefeet are designed for digging, combing fur, and handling stones, sticks, and mud in the building of dams and lodges, rather than for land travel.

Beavers are vegetarians. Twigs, roots, bark—aspen or poplar mainly—are their principal diet.

They are family animals who mate for life. Babies, two to five in a litter, stay with the family for two years before going out on their own. The entire family lives in a cozy lodge which is usually one of many lodges in the beaver colony. All share in the work of their community, adding new lodges for new additions.

As for the lodges themselves, they are along the water's edge, in the water, or preferably on an island. Sometimes burrows are used instead. Housemaking begins with a foundation about twelve feet square. This floor is carpeted with shredded wood, leaves, or soft moss. Around it are strong walls forming a domed roof of twigs, branches, and several coatings of mud. The roof is braced and made strong enough to keep out predators. When it is filled with a winter's supply of food, the lodge becomes a comfortable little fortress. There are usually two entrances about twelve inches wide. One is a tunnel with many turns to thwart underwater hunting animals. The other is a back door where wood can be brought in for food. It also serves as a quick exit.

The "busy beaver" deserves his name. When he is not building lodges, he is constructing dams. The site is usually downstream from the colony, in a stream with narrow sides and a firm bottom. Cutting begins as the workers stand on their hind legs and start gnawing two furrows around the chosen trees. In one night, a single beaver can fell a tree eight inches thick. When the tree falls, hopefully toward the water, the branches are cut off and the log gnawed into shorter lengths for easier handling. The lengths are then rolled or floated to the dam. If the forest is thin and good trees are far from the site, canals are often dug to float down the logs, sometimes as far as one hundred feet.

When the logs reach the site, they are sunk to the bottom and anchored there by stones carried from shore. On this foundation the dam is built up of smaller sticks and branches. When it is completed, it forms a half circle with the top backing into the current.

But still the work goes on. Heavy rains, ice floes make necessary constant reinforcement. Forest animals use the dam as a bridge, and like a highway, the dam must be repaired.

Why does a beaver bother to build a dam? He builds it to create deep water in which to build his lodge.

The beaver is well equipped for this underwater work. His fur is made up of long, coarse outer hair over fine, soft, waterproof underfur. Beavers often spend hours combing this fur, spreading oil from oil sacs onto the outer hairs, to keep the skin waterproof.

Beaver color ranges from tawny yellow to red-brown and even black. This thick, lush, underfur made the pelts so valuable to man that it nearly caused the destruction of the beaver in North America.

These are only a few of the mammals in the Great Lakes area. There are others—wily, strong hunters, like wolves, marten, lynx, fox; and birds, like eagles, hawks, shore and water birds, brightly plumaged songbirds; and fish, like lake trout, whitefish, sturgeon, perch, pike, and many others. Snakes run from the common harmless garter snake to the deadly copperhead and rattler. Their ranges vary, and Michigan, for example, has only one poisonous snake, the relatively small Massasauga rattler. In the fresh water are turtles —the common painted turtle, the leathery soft-shelled turtle, and the snapping turtle, moss-backed and ugly. Insects buzz or flutter—the gaily-colored dragonfly, the annoying mosquito.

This was the land that awaited the coming of yet another mammal, one who would change the face of the Great Lakes country forever. Of reddish-brown color, walking erect, he was called man.

3

MAN HIMSELF

A very long time ago, during the advances and retreats of the great glaciers, man appeared in the Great Lakes area. He had probably come from Asia's great north, slowly making his way across the Bering Straits, then down into North America. The time of his long trek was perhaps fifteen thousand years ago, perhaps longer.

These people, called Indians, were hunters and gatherers. Instead of moving as tribes, they came in small groups. Some crossed the Bering Straits on a dry-land bridge toward the end of the Ice Age. At that time, water drawn from the ocean to form the great ice caps lowered the water level in the Bering Straits as much as two or three hundred feet. The

land, relieved for a time of this great weight, probably rose. Then as the glaciers melted, the land bridge disappeared once more.

Others had to cross the straits by boat, fishing as they went. In winter still others crossed into Alaska on the ice.

Perhaps a herd of mammoth or a band of musk oxen, moving as the climate changed, first lured these tiny bands of people. With no idea of what kind of land awaited them, they followed the forests, berries, roots, wild grains, animals. Hunting and gathering for survival, they moved onward as the climate changed.

The long trip may have taken twenty years, it may have taken a thousand. For these were families with children, carrying simple weapons and tools, hunting and camping as they went. Others followed, until at last the Indians spread across both North and South America. These were the Paleo-Indians, meaning Indians of old or ancient culture. Like the animals and vegetation around them, they began adapting to their surroundings and the climate.

In appearance they varied widely. All had straight black hair and dark eyes, inherited perhaps from their Asiatic ancestors. But some were tall, some were short. Faces were broad or narrow, bodies stocky or slender. The tall hawk-nosed type was only one of many. Even their color varied from brown to reddish.

Progress was slow. They knew how to chip stone for tools and weapons, how to hunt and fish, how to build temporary shelters. But they had no tame animals except the dog. These dogs came with them. One was a medium-sized, heavily furred animal much like the Alaskan husky. The other was small and leaner, like a coyote.

Their first tools were the fluted stone points, scrapers,

bone needles, stone blades. Later came the curved throwing stick, the spear, and spear thrower.

These spear throwers, or *atlatls,* gave the Indian added distance and power. An atlatl was made by taking a short wooden rod and notching it at one end. The other end served as a handle. On this rod was placed a drilled-out stone of varying shape and weight called a banner stone. The hunter placed the butt end of his spear into the notch and grasped the rod by the handle. Drawing his arm straight back he hurled the spear with great force. Throwing spears were lighter than thrusting spears. Both types were tipped with stemmed or notched stone heads.

These stone heads or points probably offer the best clues as to the location and age of the Paleo-Indians. Carbon-14 tests show them to be from twelve to nine thousand years old, which coincides with the time of the last of the huge mammoths.

Ancient stone points are easily recognizable because of the groove or fluting running up one or both sides of the point. Shape and size varied, but all were streamlined and made to fit into the split point of the spear where they were held fast with bindings.

Because their points had no barbs, spears could be thrust deep into an animal, pulled free, and thrust in again and again.

There were three major ways of making stone points. One was to flake off small bits of stone by striking small and careful blows with a hammerstone. Later flint "knapping" came into use. Here a mallet was struck against a simple punch of bone or hardened wood. The finest points were made by the third method, where pressure was applied with a hardened wood tool to dislodge separate flakes of stone.

The Old Woodland Indians of five to eight thousand years ago invented still another means of working stone. Instead of flaking flint, they used a different hard-grained stone, pounding and pecking it into shape. When ground and polished, it furnished sleek hard tools with sharp cutting edges. Two types of axes were peculiar to this time. One was a grooved axe, the other a barbed axe found only in Michigan.

The Indian probably hunted beaver, elk, deer, caribou, and musk oxen, and possibly the mammoth as well. But because of its great size, the early elephant must first have had to be caught and held helpless in a snare or trapped by mud in the swamps. Only then could the hunters rush in with their spears, thrusting for the underbelly or between the huge ribs. Once down, the animal had to be cut on the spot and the meat packed to camp.

From about 1000 to 4000 B.C., the Old Copper Indians were also at work. These people were probably the first metal workers in the world. They worked in the Lake Superior region along Michigan's northern shore. Thousands of pits were dug along the top of Michigan's Upper Peninsula as well as on Isle Royale in Lake Superior.

To find the copper, these early miners traced the veins of pure copper showing on surface rocks down into the ground. Pits were dug and the rocks heated, then chilled suddenly with water. The copper was then broken out by hammering with boulders or prying with wooden levers. Taken to camp, the copper was made into tools, ornaments, and weapons. Shaping was done by hammering, heating, and chilling the metal to keep it from becoming brittle.

Typical objects that they made were spear points, knives, fishhooks, and harpoons. Their tools were axes or flat adzes for woodworking, attached to wood or antler-bone handles.

Gouges, chisels, punches, and needles were made also. Ornaments were rare and usually were beads in tubed or round shapes, as well as bracelets and pendants. Other tools were formed by stone or bone. They made bird-bone whistles, shell beads, containers and perhaps canoes from the bark of the white or paper birch.

A common canoe type was the dugout. This was formed by hollowing out a log into a boat by means of burning and shaping with axes, adzes, and scrapers.

Homes for both the Old Woodland and Old Copper groups were sapling frames, round-topped, covered with sheets of bark, skin, or mats. They were easy to erect and could be left behind with little loss when the family moved.

With the climate change of three thousand years ago, many of these Indians began moving northward. Others remained in the south and became a part of the Woodland Indians. As for the working of copper, it died out about 1000 B.C. and was only revived briefly by later peoples, such as the Hopewell Indians and the Late Woodland groups.

Then about 500 B.C., there appeared yet another group. Because they built huge round-topped mounds above their dead, they are called the Mound Builders.

Apparently the dead were first placed on platforms or in trees to keep their bodies safe from roving animals. When it was time to build, weapons, tools, ornaments, and red ocher (a red rock powder), were put with the corpses in a shallow grave. Then basket after basket of earth or silt was piled over the graves, forming a high mound. Some builders farther to the south made these mounds in the shapes of animals.

Because of the great effort to make them and the wealth put into the tombs for use in the spirit world, probably only the more important members of the tribe received this special treatment.

Another gift of these early peoples was the making of pottery. Early types were thick, broad-mouthed jars with designs pressed into the wet clay by fabrics or cords. There were thin jars, as well, decorated on the rims or the body. This type of pottery was probably first made in the northern forests of Europe and Asia. From there it seems to have spread to the northern forests of North America and was carried clear to the Atlantic.

One of the most advanced of the Mound Builders were the Hopewell Indians. These people lived for more than five hundred years in the Mississippi, Ohio, and Illinois river valleys. As the climate grew warmer, they moved by boat to the north and into the Great Lakes region. These people preferred open hardwood forests with a warm climate, because they were farmers as well as hunters and fishermen. Their crops were chiefly corn, squash, sunflowers for seeds, and perhaps tobacco.

From their skeletons and some small sculptured figures found in the mounds, they appear to have been of medium height, longheaded, stocky, with oval faces and "slanting" eyes. The men wore breechcloths, the women wraparound skirts of hide or woven material. Both wore moccasins. Men wore their hair long in back and gathered into a knot, with only a forelock left in front. Women's hair was worn long, parted in the middle and drawn back above the ears.

The Hopewells brought the first agriculture, and they also brought trade to the Great Lakes area. From the southern Atlantic coasts they received large marine shells, which they used for dishes. From the Rocky Mountains came a hard black rock called obsidian, from which they made ceremonial knives. From the southern Appalachians came mica, often used for primitive mirrors. Copper and silver came from the mines of Lake Superior, lead from Illinois and Missouri.

These remarkable Indians also made musical instruments. Flutes were used, made from three or four hollow tubes of bone or reed of different lengths, bound together with bands of copper or silver. When blown upon, they gave off notes of varying pitch. Accompanying these pipes were drums, as well as rattles often made from carved turtle shells. Tobacco pipes had spool or barrel-shaped bowls. Made from polished stone, they were often carved in the shape of people or animals.

They were also skilled artists; they made fine pottery, polished stone and copper ornaments. Even bear's teeth were inlaid with river pearls for necklaces. As artisans they were never equaled by any other Indian tribe in North America.

From the time of the development of the Old Copper Indians to the time of the Mound Builders took about five hundred years. For the next fifteen hundred, the Woodland Indians developed into peoples of many tribes and languages. From what may have been one language, they now began dividing into language groups who spoke as many as 150 languages.

These Indians hunted, fished, planted, traded, and fought. All had a religious life, burial ceremonies, community and tribal customs.

Various spirits or gods were worshipped. Called *Manitous* by the Algonquian peoples, with *Gitchi Manitous* the supreme being, these spirits were believed to govern success in hunting, farming, the relief of illness, the winning of a battle. There were evil spirits as well as those who worked tricks or pranks. Spirits were thought to have invented nets for fishing, fire, even the earth. Their legends told of a great flood, of the formation of the earth on the back of a monstrous turtle.

Animals, too, had magical powers. Upon reaching manhood, boys were left alone in the woods to fast and dream. The animal which appeared to a boy in a dream would become his guardian or *totem* forever. Should he be forced to kill this animal for food, he made a sacrifice of tobacco to its spirit and begged its forgiveness.

Indians made offerings to their gods as well. But these gifts were not in return for past favors; instead they were made to insure future help.

Places were also sacred. Strange-shaped rocks were the homes of spirits or giants. Trees, rivers, even the stars themselves were spirits.

Some of the Indians were wanderers. Most spent their lives in towns or villages. Houses ranged from the bark-covered wigwams of the Algonquian to the well-built, many-familied dwellings of the Iroquois which were called longhouses. Often these villages were protected from attack by sharpened log palisades or walls. Still, the Woodland Indians never shaped timbers or set stone into any sort of permanent dwellings.

By now, tribes were made up of a few hundred or several thousand people. Loosely bound together, they moved about or in some cases lived in a certain area for centuries. If they stayed in one section for a long time, most members became blood relatives. In some tribes, all male relatives of the father—uncles and grandfather—were called father by the children. The mother's sisters, mother, and grandmothers were called mother.

Languages changed until separate tribes could not understand each other even though they had all started with a common tongue.

Without a written language, the Indians used belts made up of beads or shells strung on thongs. Called *wampum,* these belts could, by their design and color, carry a message. Later, the belts were used as money.

Within the tribes were smaller groups called clans. Each clan had its totem and name from some animal—the wolf clan, turtle, loon, bear, beaver. Among the Iroquois, children belonged to the clan of the mother. Among the Algonquian, the father's clan was the children's clan. Marriage within the same clan was forbidden.

As for death, it meant passing into the spirit world, a world not too far away where game and food were plentiful. The spirits of this other world were believed to have great powers. In daily living, the Late Woodland Indians had changed very little from their ancestors. They were still hunters. Deer were their principal game, furnishing both food and hides for the making of clothing. Many were fishermen and gatherers of the wild rice that reached from Lake Michigan to Lake Superior.

War, hunting, fishing, the making of canoes—these were men's work. Gathering, tending crops, house building, and the making of clothing and baskets were women's work. The dog was still their only tame animal, helping in hunting or, in some tribes, serving as a favorite food. For travel the Indian used the swift birch-bark canoe. Some canoes were great war canoes carrying twelve or more men. Others were small one-man types, light and easy to carry on land around rough water, rocks, or falls, such as the mighty cataract of Niagara.

In the village itself, life was busy. Arrow makers chipped at the flint, often telling the old legends of the tribe's greatness or the power of the Manitous. The atlatl had been exchanged for the bow and arrow. Some of the flint for points came from flint quarries south of Lake Erie. The women busied themselves making baskets from wooden splints or sewing deerskin garments decorated with porcupine quills dyed in many colors. Designs were of flowers and leaves twining themselves in bright-colored patterns. There was corn to be ground into meal, venison to be smoked to last the family through the long winter months when game was scarce. In the spring the sugar maples were tapped for sap to be boiled down into syrup and sugar in huge moose-hide kettles.

If there was work, there was play as well. Most sports were tests of skill and strength that helped train the young men for the hunt and for war. One such game, called La Crosse today, was named *bagataway*. Two teams lined up to defend their goal posts, each member carrying curved basket-ended sticks. A ball was then tossed and fought after by both teams in an attempt to throw or carry the ball past the opposing team's goal. Rough and rugged, it called for great speed and staying power.

As for the children, they practiced with the bow and arrow or played games, such as the moccasin game. Here one player laid five moccasins face down. Under one he slipped a stone. The other player then had to guess where the stone lay. Adults liked the game as well, often betting heavily on the outcome.

But the most serious game was war. It, too, had certain rules. Sometimes the attacker would notify his enemy of the coming invasion by sending a sheaf of arrows or a wampum belt painted scarlet.

INDIAN TRIBES and FRENCH
EXPLORERS ∴ 1634 – 1681

N

QUEBEC

MONTREAL

OTTAWA

HURON

L. Ontario

IROQUOIS

NEUTRAL

NIAGARA FALLS

CO. SCHOOLS
C688588

Erie.

ERIE

Routes of the Explorers
Nicolet ------
La Salle ....
Marquette-Jolliet ━━━
Menard ✓ ✓ ✓ ✓

There were two basic types of warfare. One was to protect home and family, the other to make raids or expeditions to avenge injury or take spoils and captives.

As forest Indians, they fought from the cover of trees. War chiefs might direct part of the action but most combat was hand-to-hand. If a fortified village was attacked, flaming arrows were used to drive out the defenders.

To die in battle was thought to be one of the best ways to end life. Still, the Indian did not believe in fighting against overwhelming numbers and preferred to slip away to fight again. As for the victors, they returned to their village carrying the scalps of the slain as trophies. Shouting, applauding, the village turned out to greet them and to torment the captives. Captured warriors were forced to undergo terrible tortures until they died, perhaps days later. This furnished amusement for the villagers as well as proving the bravery of the vanquished. Should the captive undergo fire, knife, hatchet without a murmur, he achieved greatness. Then among some tribes, parts of his body, including his heart, were eaten by the captors so that they might become equally brave. Many captives were kept as slaves and finally adopted into the tribe.

By the time the first Europeans arrived, a wide Indian population surrounded the Great Lakes. These tribes were divided into three large language groups—Algonquian, Iroquoian, and Siouxian.

The most powerful and the best organized were the Iroquois, living along the eastern shores of Lake Ontario. Powerful warriors, they were the bitter enemy of the Algonquian peoples.

Below Lake Erie were the Eries, an Iroquoian group. The northern shores were a sort of neutral hunting ground. On the western shore of Lake Huron lived the Tionontati and Hurons, also Iroquoian. The rest of the Great Lakes area was inhabited by Algonquian peoples—except for the Winnebago, who were linked to the western Sioux. On Lake Michigan's western shore lived the Kickapoo, Sac, Menomini, and Fox. Above Lake Superior were the Ojibwa (Ojibway or Chippewa), one of the largest nations north of Mexico, numbering 25,000 or more. Along the shores of Lake Huron lived the Ottawa. Between Lakes Huron and Michigan, the Potawatomi. Of common language stock, the Ottawa, Ojibwa, and Potawatomi joined in a sort of loose confederacy calling themselves the Three Fires. South, in Indiana, were the Miami; in Illinois were found the Kaskaskia and Peoria tribes.

It was from these people that the European would learn the way of the wilderness. He would depend on the Indian to furnish the swift birch-bark canoe to carry him on his explorations and trade routes. Indian snowshoes would help him walk over deep snow during the bitter winter months. He would follow their ancient trails, trails so well-planned that they still exist as modern highways. They would eat the Indian's basic food—corn—use the plants and fruits, tap the maples for the sweet maple sugar. Indian words would come into his language—wigwam, succotash, hominy, canoe, maize, tobacco, moccasin. And finally states would bear the names of the once-proud tribes or would have names with Indian meanings, like Minnesota, Wisconsin, Illinois, Michigan, Ohio. Lakes would become Michigan, Huron, Erie. Cities were to be called Chicago, Muskegon, and thousands of other Indian names.

For the Indian, the long trek of fifteen thousand years or more was over. During those years he had learned to live with cold, hunger, even war. But now a new force had come from across the sea, a force that would use the Indian in trade and in war ... then take his lands and nearly destroy him.

4

BLACK ROBES AND
BEAVER PELTS

The Indians waited, amazed. Some squatted on the beach, others knelt or stood, gazing at these strange creatures who had come ashore. Who were these men with pale skins and hair upon their faces? As if in answer, the leader strode forward. Plumes waved above the broad-brimmed hat shadowing his face, moustached and bearded, framed by shoulder-length dark hair worn in the French style. But instead of a many-buttoned, cuffed, and braided coat, he wore the gorgeous robes of an oriental emperor. In each hand he held a long-barreled pistol.

This was Jean Nicolet, explorer for His Excellency, Samuel de Champlain, explorer, soldier, and governor of New

France. The year was 1634. Nicolet had been sent here to find a dream—a dream that would haunt explorers and kings for years to come. It was that of finding a water route across the unknown west—a route that could lead them to Asia and the gold of Cathay.

The first Europeans to see the Great Lakes in their search were Étienne Brulé and his friend Grenoble. Also sent by Champlain, they had lived first among the Huron tribes near Georgian Bay, learning their language and customs. Then, with the friendly Hurons as guides, they had set out to explore the country.

From Georgian Bay they swung west, hugging the rocky shore until they reached the foaming rapids called *Sault* (soo) by the French. And beyond the racing waters feeding into Lake Huron, they saw for the first time mighty Lake Superior.

When their story reached Champlain, his hopes for a waterway rose even higher. So sure was he that the route would lead to Asia that he presented Nicolet with a brilliant silk robe so that he might make a fitting appearance before the Chinese emperor himself.

Now, dressed in this flowing silk, Nicolet looked about him at the clustered Indians. Some wore hunting shirts of fringed buckskin, painted with the designs of animals, decorated with dyed porcupine quills and moose hair. Others were naked except for breechclouts. All had thick black hair rising in a high roach above their painted and shaved heads. All wore one or more black-tipped eagle feathers. Around their necks were strung shells, bear claws, bits of copper. Some even had pendants in their noses.

Slowly Jean Nicolet raised his pistols and pulled the triggers. Flint struck steel, powder flashed in the pans, the guns flashed and roared. A great murmur ran through the crowd of red men. This indeed must be a god who held thunder and lightning in both hands!

But to Nicolet, the moment was filled with disappointment. He had failed to find the Northwest Passage.

What he didn't realize was that soon others would follow him through the Straits of Mackinac. And in a short time the region would yield wealth rivaling that of Cathay herself—not gold, but furs. And furs were easy to carry back to Montreal and Quebec, where a ready market waited in Europe. These furs would yield tremendous profits, for their only price would be a few handfuls of cheap trade goods. And the French were there first. At this time, Britain had only two settlements in the New World, at Plymouth and Jamestown. The Great Lakes area was French alone.

Champlain knew it was important to keep friends among the tribes. To prove his friendship, he had even engaged in two fierce battles with the dreaded Iroquois, the enemies of the Algonquian people. But because of the unfriendly Iroquois, only the Upper Peninsula could be explored for the present. The lands around Lake Ontario at the beginning of the southern route through the Lakes were Iroquois country. For now, they must paddle the more difficult northern route to reach Lakes Huron, Michigan, and Superior.

This route began at Quebec. Long canoes, paddled by the colorful *voyageurs,* made their way up the St. Lawrence River, then plunged into the treacherous Ottawa River. Here, rapids were dangerous and plentiful, requiring as many as thirty-six *portages,* or land carries, before reaching Lake Nipissing. From there the going was easier, paddling down the French River and into Georgian Bay. Coasting past the bark wigwams of the friendly Hurons on their left, they could follow the North Channel between the northern shore and Manitoulin Island. Or they could bear left into Lake Michigan and on to Green Bay.

Traveling with the brigades of canoes were the missionaries, called "black robes" by the Indians. For the French King had proclaimed that exploration and the Church must go hand in hand. To these missionaries, this was a heaven-sent opportunity to bring Christianity to the Indians. They pursued their task with great courage and zeal. Many suffered torture and death at the hands of hostile tribes. But they kept on, preaching, hoping, giving out silver crosses to all who would listen and believe. Their hopes were never completely fulfilled. Still, the journals of these educated and determined men proved to be invaluable to those who would follow in opening up this unknown land.

As for the growing trade, the French, like the Dutch and English to the east, cheated the Indian. But unlike the Dutch and English, they were able to make friends. Not only did they take the trouble to learn the languages, they even adopted the clothing for easier movement in the woods. Many married into the tribes.

In order to carry out the fur trade, a man who wished to go "furring" first needed permission from the governor in Quebec. In return, he carried the missionaries with him. He also engaged voyageurs to paddle his fleet of canoes, as well as *coureurs de bois,* woods rangers, to hunt and trap.

The voyageurs were a hardy and colorful group, recruited mostly from the area around Quebec and the Gaspé Peninsula. Boisterous, quick-tempered, proud, they were also able to paddle for seemingly limitless hours with only a handful of dried corn or peas and a little pork or venison. The best canoemen were short, with powerful arms and shoulders.

The canoes, of Indian design, were made from the bark of a single white birch sewn into strips with red spruce root.

This bark was then stretched over a skeleton frame made from white cedar. The smallest, called the Indian canoe, was lightweight and was fifteen feet long. North canoes were twenty-five feet long, while the huge Montreal canoes were a full forty feet in length. Pointed at both ends, they were up to six feet wide at the center. Narrow bars or thwarts across the top kept the canoe in shape. Below the gunwales were hung four-inch-wide boards on which the kneeling canoe-men rested. In the large canoes, six men in the middle—three on each side—worked with two foot paddles. At the stern was the steersman, at the bow the bowman, each with longer, wider paddles. Passengers, trade goods, supplies were stowed in the remaining space. On the return trip, furs were made up into ninety-pound bales and piled high. A single voyageur might pick up two of these bales and wade to shore.

Distances traveled were not measured in miles but in "pipes." At given times, the long brigade would pause to rest. It was then time for the men to fill their clay pipes with tobacco from colorfully-decorated tobacco pouches or from pouches formed at the end of their long-tailed stocking caps. A journey then might be a short twenty-pipe journey, or a long one-hundred-pipe one.

Clothing was a mixture of French *habitant*—as the French-Canadian settlers were called—and Indian. On the head was a stocking cap, usually blue. In it was thrust a feather, the mark of a true "man of the north," of which they were very proud. Full-cut shirts of homespun reached nearly to the knees. At the waist, they wore long, brilliantly colored sashes tied at the back. Leggings were pure Indian in design, made of buckskin or cloth, often fringed. Decorated bands held them tight just below the knee. With the leggings they wore the Indian breechclout, which hung down in front and in back. On their feet they wore moccasins. In winter, they wore a heavy coat made from a blanket, sometimes with a hood. Hair fell to the shoulders; moustaches or full beards were common. They were usually fond of music and singing, and had many canoe songs to help them keep the paddle rhythm of forty strokes to the minute.

For trade goods, they first brought items of their own that they thought the Indians would like. Steel axes, combs, bright cloth, hawk's bells that jingled, mirrors, scissors. What matter if the Indian wore the scissors as a hair ornament? Then as furring grew brisk, items were manufactured specially for the Indian. Now he could have trade muskets, steel tomahawk heads, vermilion paint, trade beads, kettles, small metal cones to be fastened to buckskin fringe, called "tinkling cones."

In return, the trader received beaver, otter, and other furs taken in the winter when the fur was thickest. Stored until spring, the furs were then loaded into canoes for the return trip to Montreal or Quebec. From there they were shipped to the European market.

Prices for pelts varied. But a trader's journal lists the following: One trade musket, twenty beaver. Trade blanket (varying weights were measured by points and marked on the hem), ten skins. An axe, three; half pint of gunpowder, one; ten musket balls, one; rum or brandy, one or two skins, depending on how much it had been watered down.

This last item, more than any other, helped to destroy the Indian. In spite of the threats and pleadings of missionaries, traders depended on rum to help in the trading. Soon the Indian demanded the "white man's milk." Unable to handle the powerful liquor, the Indian sometimes found himself trading all he owned for a single keg. As a result, murders grew common; massacres were to follow.

Before the trader, the Indian hunted only for his own

needs. Now he killed all the game he could, in order to trade for trinkets, a gun, or a tomahawk. Before long many of the tribes gave up all activities except hunting. Finally they became dependent on the white man for clothing and even food.

Meanwhile, the missionaries were doing their best to establish missions. Most were Jesuits; some, like Father Jogues, met horrible deaths at the hands of the Iroquois. The Iroquois, determined to drive out the French, began raiding far from their own hunting grounds. The Hurons near Georgian Bay were attacked and forced to flee to the west end of Lake Superior. In 1622 the Iroquois met and defeated a war party of Ottawa and Ojibwa in the Lake Superior region.

But in spite of hostile Indians, rum, and the wilderness, the Jesuits stayed. By 1668 there were two missions established, one in Wisconsin built by Father Ménard; the second at the Sault Ste. Marie, built by Father Dablon and Father Marquette.

It was at the Sault that Father Marquette first heard of a great river flowing south, possibly into the Gulf of California. Determined to check the truth of the story, Father Marquette began making plans for further exploration. But before he could leave, Indians at the mission murdered several Sioux. Fearing revenge from these fierce Plains warriors, the Hurons and Ottawas ran south to the shore of Lake Michigan. Marquette had no choice but to follow and establish a new mission at the tip of Michigan's Upper Peninsula above the Straits, called St. Ignace. Soon this became an important meeting place for traders and Indians alike.

Finally in 1673 Father Marquette was ready to undertake his journey down the mighty Mississippi. With the explorer Jolliet and five men, he traveled the Fox and Wisconsin Rivers to the Mississippi. A long journey took them south to the mouth of the Arkansas River. All were convinced that this was truly the river which flowed into the Gulf. Returning to Green Bay, Father Marquette, tired and ill, tried one more visit to his Indians in Illinois. On his return, he died on the eastern shore of Lake Michigan and was buried at the present city of Ludington.

Next to travel down the Mississippi was Robert Cavelier, Sieur de La Salle. His plan was to build a chain of forts that would keep the English from moving in. To provide funds, he planned to gather many furs. Instead of sending them back by canoe, he chose instead to build a small sailing vessel on the banks of the Niagara River. Boasting five small cannon and a carved figurehead, she was named the *Griffin*.

A temporary defeat by French soldiers had caused the Iroquois to sign a treaty of peace. Travel on the lower Great Lakes was now possible.

This lower route, unless there were storms, was far easier than the northern one. First taken by the French explorer Ménard, the route began at Quebec, then up the St. Lawrence to Lake Ontario, then a portage around Niagara Falls into Lake Erie. From there canoes could steer through the Detroit River, Lake St. Clair, the St. Clair River, and finally into Lake Huron.

By building his vessel above the falls, La Salle was able to launch her into Lake Erie and by August 7, 1679, the first sailing vessel on the Great Lakes had begun her journey.

To the amazement of the Indians, this "great white bird" moved swiftly without paddles across Lake Erie. She reached the Detroit River and made her way safely into Lake Huron. Here she met a violent storm but managed to reach St. Ignace at last.

At the Straits she again caused much excitement to the dwellers at *Michilimackinac*. This name was used for the entire Straits area, including Mackinac Island. The rough translation of the word is "Place of the dancing turtle spirits."

After a brief rest, the *Griffin* set sail for the entrance to Green Bay. Here she took on a full load of furs. La Salle directed her captain to sail for Niagara, unload, then meet him and a small body of men on the St. Joseph River. The *Griffin* departed; La Salle and his crew set out by canoe toward Michigan's western shore. At the St. Joseph River, they built Fort Miami. When the *Griffin* failed to arrive, they moved on to the Illinois River and built another fort. Upon La Salle's return, he learned that the *Griffin* was lost. Probably sunk by storms, her fate remains a mystery of the Lakes.

Without a ship, La Salle was faced with a thousand-mile journey on foot in order to reach Canada. Again filled with determination, the little band set out. Living off the land, they finally reached their destination.

Then in December of 1681, La Salle was back at Fort Miami and ready to embark down the Mississippi with thirty-one Indians and twenty-three Frenchmen. This time, the group actually reached the Gulf of Mexico, proving Father Marquette's theory about the great river.

In 1687, La Salle raised a small fleet and attempted to find the mouth of the river from the gulf. But there was dissatisfaction among his followers, and La Salle was killed.

Next, Sieur Duluth, under a new governor, made peace between the Michigan and Wisconsin Indians and the Sioux of the west. For the first time the broad new lands west of Lake Superior were open to exploration.

A new fort had also been built between Lake Huron and Lake Erie, called Fort St. Joseph. In spite of this, eleven British canoes reached Michilimackinac. Here, to their surprise, they found the Indians eager to trade for the cheaper

Michigan Tourist Council

Fort Michilimackinac reconstruction in an early stage. The high log palisade walls and blockhouses are typical of frontier forts. Top center shows the land gate and ball field where Pontiac's warriors gathered to capture the fort from the British.

British goods. But it was their last trip, for the traders were captured by the French on their return.

Now, the time of conflict neared. While the French had been furring in the wilds, marrying into the tribes, becoming wilderness dwellers, the British had been building colonies. For allies, they had the powerful Iroquois. To combat this threat, the French built more forts at important sites. At St. Ignace was Fort de Buade. Below Fort Miami, they built another Fort St. Joseph.

In 1689, France and England declared war. In French Canada, Governor Frontenac appointed a proud and ambitious young man as commandant of Fort de Buade and head of all of the forts in the northwest. His name was Antoine de la Mothe Cadillac.

Fort de Buade at St. Ignace was the most important post in the Great Lakes area. During the trading season, the fort and the grounds were crowded with over five thousand Indians and hundreds of coureurs de bois. There was also a French village of sixty houses as well as a town of Hurons and a town of Ottawas. Before long, the great volume of trade in furs brought a lowering of prices at Montreal.

But the missionaries continued to press their case, demanding that the Indians be protected from the traders and their rum.

Finally, in 1696, King Louis XIV closed the west to trade. None but missionaries would be allowed in the villages; the Indians would have to carry their furs eastward to market.

This was a cruel blow to the traders and to Cadillac. As commandant he had made a fortune in furs, as well as serving as peacemaker among the tribes. He would need another post.

In a daring plan, Cadillac proposed that he be allowed to build a new post between Lake St. Clair and Lake Erie. It could be supported by fur profits and would be an important link in the chain being forged to keep out the British.

Governor Frontenac listened. Knowing of Cadillac's earlier success, he gave his permission for Cadillac to sail for Paris and the King. He received the King's approval for his plan, and returned to Canada.

Cadillac's first trip to set up the new post was a success. In 1701, he left Montreal with one hundred coureurs de bois and regular soldiers and one hundred Indians. On July 24, his twenty-five canoes reached the Detroit River. There, on a level stretch of ground above high clay banks and surrounded by water on three sides, they built Fort Pontchartrain. From this position Cadillac knew that his guns could sweep the narrow river and defeat any British fleet that might attack.

Its construction was typical of forest forts. It was built of log palisades twelve feet high, crowned by blockhouses, that surrounded log houses. It even had a church, Ste. Anne's, the patron saint of voyageurs.

Back in Montreal, however, there was jealousy of Cadillac's power. Soon rumors were spreading. The new fort was only temporary, they said. Settlers and Indians would be foolish to go there.

But Cadillac was not to be stopped. In a surprise move, to prove the strength of the post, he sent for his wife and their six-year-old son. Traveling by canoe through Iroquois country, they arrived safely in 1701. Settlers and Indians cheered. The post was to be permanent after all.

Now at Cadillac's invitation, Indians began arriving from Michilimackinac in such numbers that the mission there was abandoned. Ottawa and Ojibwa built villages above the fort; Hurons and Miamis below.

Next, Cadillac asked permission to build an Indian school

and to train the Indians as soldiers. Both requests were denied, for fear the Indians in their new knowledge might turn against the French.

Still, the tribes remained loyal. Much of this was due to Cadillac himself. He was careful to follow Indian custom and formalities. Visiting chiefs received presents of lace, gold braid, red coats, vermilion, tobacco, and, of course, brandy.

Another practice he followed was the use of Indian wampum. And when addressing the chiefs he called them "My Children." They in turn addressed him as "Our Father." At council fires he smoked the peace pipe, or calumet, sharing it with the others.

Cadillac had hoped to become a *seigneur,* a landholder. This would have given him rights over the settlers or habitants. Then, not only must they have had to raise their hats to him, but they would have had to work a few days a year on his farm, pay him to grind their grain, and to rent their own lands.

Failing this, Cadillac was given the power to rent lands to others. Soon long strips of land called ribbon farms spread along the river banks. Within the stockade were sixty-eight small lots, outside, seventy-five farms. Rent was paid in furs or cash. Then, Cadillac imported cattle and horses. Pigs were kept on an island to protect them from wolves.

Without roads, the only means of travel was by canoe. But with canoes, the habitant could not only carry grain and produce to the fort, he could head north or east, traveling hundreds of miles with comparative ease.

Still, the settlement remained relatively small. The French had failed to match stride with the increasing British population. Part of this was due to the lack of religious freedom. Only Roman Catholics were allowed in New France. Protestant Frenchmen, the Huguenots, were eager to come but permission was denied. In addition, the climate was harsh; the only product was furs, so trading was relatively limited.

But the British colonies had a wide variety of climate and products to offer, as well as religious freedom. Land was easy to come by, and settlers arrived by the thousands.

Again, land, water, climate were having their effect, this time on the European settlers of North America.

From 1680 to 1763, the French and British fought four wars on both continents. In the French and Indian War which lasted from 1754 to 1760, the English found themselves facing increasingly powerful forts. Among them were Fort Ticonderoga, a massive stone fortress high above Lake Champlain. Fort Niagara, also of heavy stone, commanded the all-important waterway leading westward. A new fort had been built at the Sault, as well as one at the northern tip of Michigan, Fort Michilimackinac. Another line of posts ran from Lake Erie to the forks of the Ohio.

In 1754, Major George Washington was ordered into the Ohio country with demands that the French leave. Receiving a firm "No," he attempted to build a fort on the forks of the Ohio, only to have his advance troops soundly defeated. The French and Indian War had begun.

Immediately, the French built a fort of their own called Fort Duquesne. In 1755, General Braddock attempted its capture. In the battle that followed, his forces were crushed, he himself was killed.

Elsewhere the French were also victorious. Under the brilliant leadership of men like Montcalm, the regulars, militia, coureurs de bois, and Indians won victory after victory.

Then in 1758, the tide of battle turned. All supplies to New France were cut off by British ships. Fort Duquesne was captured, as well as the great stone fortresses of Ticonderoga, Niagara and Crown Point.

The most crushing blow was the defeat of French forces on the Plains of Abraham at Quebec. Both the British General Wolfe, and and the French General Montcalm, were killed. Only Montreal remained. And on September 8, 1760, attacked on three sides, Montreal surrendered.

The dream of a New France was shattered, and Britain was the victor.

Major Robert Rogers, famed leader of the Royal Rangers, was sent to take over the French posts. With two hundred rangers, traveling by whaleboat, he made his way westward to Detroit. Down came the white flag of France, in its place fluttered the Union Jack of Britain. In post after post, clear to Michilimackinac, the French soldiers climbed aboard bateaux and left. In their place, the French Canadians waited. So did the Indians. What would these new conquerors bring to the land of the Great Lakes?

5

TRADE MUSKET
AND TOMAHAWK

There seemed to be little difference at first between the British traders and their red-coated soldiers, and the French who had left. British goods were lower in price; the traders were eager for furs. The Canadians appeared to agree with the Indians' opinions. It was business as usual.

In Detroit, Captain Donald Campbell and his officers readily accepted invitations for parties and balls held by the wealthier French merchants. The merchants and their ladies in turn attended Campbell's parties with pleasure.

Far to the north at Fort Michilimackinac, trade also prospered. There were several British traders at the fort as well as twenty-eight soldiers of the Royal American Regiment,

the 60th Foot, under Lieutenant William Leslye. Other garrisons held Fort Miami, Green Bay, Ouiatenon in Indiana, and a new fort at Sandusky, Ohio.

Then in 1762, reinforcements were sent to the western posts. Captain Etherington went to Michilimackinac, Lieutenant John Jamet to Sault Ste. Marie.

The officers' quarters were comfortable, their tables set with fine china and silver sent from England. But for the enlisted man, life was boring and lonely, interrupted only by drills or doses of harsh discipline. Deserters or drunkards met instant and brutal punishment. Some were forced to straddle a tall wooden horse while heavy muskets were tied to each foot and their hands were lashed behind their backs. Without food or water, they suffered in full view of the garrison. For others, pillories or stocks clamped necks and wrists, or ankles. Cruelest of all was the whipping post, where men might receive as many as a thousand lashes, actually a death sentence! Women who misbehaved were thrust into a wooden cage called a whirligig. By means of ropes, the cage was whirled at high speed. Sometimes the victims went insane.

Times were harsh. Trade rum brought about fights; knifings were common. Finally, General Amherst ordered the traders to stop giving the Indians ball and powder. The Indians were stunned. This had always been part of French trading. More and more dependent upon the musket, they wondered how they might hunt. The Long Knives, as they called the British, wanted them to starve!

There was growing Indian unrest also from the loss of their lands to the settlers. Ownership of land was something the Indian could not understand. To him the French merely used his lands, and he was still free to move about as he liked. Suddenly, the British were taking lands and punishing any Indian who trespassed on the property. Nor could the Indian understand how the French King could have given *their* lands to the British King. It was Indian land, hunted and lived upon by them for uncounted generations.

In western Pennsylvania and New York, the Delawares, Shawnees, and Senecas watched the flood of settlers with growing anger. Meanwhile, dishonest traders were robbing and cheating the Indians, unchecked by the British rulers.

Sensing this growing hostility, the remaining French began fanning the flames of rebellion. Soon, they said, the Great French Father would awaken from his sleep, and the rivers and lakes would be black with war canoes and French soldiers.

Then, above Detroit, an Ottawa chief seized the flame and lighted a torch. His name was Pontiac. Brooding in his bark wigwam, he began making plans to drive out the English forever. The first to go would be the haughty Major Gladwin, commandant of Fort Detroit. Then other forts would follow until the entire frontier was ablaze. To carry out a campaign would mean that the braves could no longer fight in the old manner—a strike here or there, then time off to fish or hunt. This time they must work together. But to unite the tribes would be difficult. There were many old tribal rivalries to overcome.

The first to come to the summons of the wampum belt were the nearby Hurons and Potawatomi. In secret council, Pontiac used his gift of oratory to great effect. Passionately, he listed the long history of wrongs they had suffered. The time of the tomahawk was at hand! The painted chiefs and warriors listened and grew even angrier. Yes, they would wait for Pontiac's signal and join in driving out the hated British.

Carefully, Pontiac outlined the plot. He and his Ottawa

would approach the fort and ask for a council. All would wear blankets hiding sawed-off muskets, scalping knives, tomahawks. Behind them would be their women also carrying hidden weapons. Outside the Potawatomi and Hurons would conceal themselves to capture any who might escape.

To his own Ottawa, the signal to attack would be when he turned up the green side of the wampum belt which he would be presenting to Gladwin. They were then to drop their blankets and strike, swiftly and hard. It was late when the council broke up. Sworn to secrecy, the braves slipped homeward.

But someone talked. Some say it was the lovely Indian girl Catherine, in love with Gladwin, who betrayed Pontiac. Others claim William Tucker, Indian-raised, heard it from his sister and passed the word to the commandant. Or the settlers may have become suspicious when the braves began borrowing files to shorten their musket barrels. In any case, Gladwin was ready.

On May 7, 1763, Pontiac with ten chiefs, sixty braves and women strode into Fort Detroit. To their amazement the entire garrison was under arms. Pontiac had no choice but to parley, holding the wampum belt white side up. Finally they left. Furious, Pontiac demanded to know who had betrayed him. No one knew, but the girl Catherine was severely beaten.

Next morning, Pontiac again entered the fort. This time he had only three chiefs at his side. Now he asked that Major Gladwin meet and receive his warriors so that all might smoke the calumet and discuss peace. The major agreed, providing that only chiefs be allowed. But the next morning when Pontiac crossed the river with the entire Ottawa village, Gladwin ordered the gates barred.

Now Pontiac ordered his camp moved two miles above

the fort. He had decided on a tactic completely foreign to Indian-type warfare. They would set siege to the fort and starve the defenders out.

Early the next morning, hordes of braves stripped to their breechclouts, painted their faces and bodies, and singing their death song advanced on Detroit. One small band killed and scalped a woman and her two sons on their farm behind the fort. Another murdered five settlers on Isle aux Cochons, where Cadillac had once kept pigs. The main force crept close to the fort and commenced firing.

By now Pontiac's forces had swollen to eight hundred men. In addition, many Frenchmen sided with the Indians and furnished them with food and advice. Thus began the longest siege in the history of Indian warfare.

Gladwin's force numbered a hundred soldiers and a handful of merchants. He had several small cannon as well as two small armed vessels, the *Huron* and *Michigan,* guarding the river. But provisions were low. Still, there was a shipment expected soon from Fort Niagara. With luck he could send back for reinforcements.

Meanwhile the entire region west of the Alleghenies was reeling under the onslaught of the tribes. Although Pontiac was chief only in the Detroit River region, the word had gone out to other tribes.

On May 16, Fort Sandusky fell. St. Joseph fell on the 25th, Miami two days later and on June 1, Fort Ouiatenon was taken. In Pennsylvania, other forts gave up to the hordes of Delaware, Seneca, and Shawnee.

Most had been taken by surprise. The strategy that failed at Detroit worked perfectly at St. Joseph. A visiting group of Potawatomi were received calmly by Ensign Schlosser. Then shots rang out. Schlosser was captured, nine soldiers killed, the others taken prisoner.

Here on the beach on Michigan's Mackinac Island in 1891 Indians still made their summer camps as their ancestors had done before them.

One of the few forts not yet under attack was Fort Michilimackinac. A busy post, it now held barracks, officers' quarters, storehouse, church, warehouses, all surrounded by a strong twenty-foot palisade. In the blockhouses cannon commanded both gates and the walls. There were three officers, thirty-five men, and several traders there.

On June 2, the day was warm. Behind the fort the Straits of Mackinac shimmered peacefully in the sun. On the horizon lay St. Ignace; to the west the island of Mackinac lay, looking like the huge turtle whose name it bore.

Only the traders sensed danger. For days the Indians had been filing in to look at the trade goods, but there had been very little trading. Instead they examined the merchandise, grunted, and left. Alexander Henry warned Captain Etherington but the commandant ignored him. As the rumors grew, Etherington threatened the next talebearer with banishment to Detroit, little knowing that Detroit lay under siege.

As for the soldiers themselves, they were looking forward eagerly to the game scheduled that day between the Ojibwa and some visiting Sac. The game was the exciting and noisy bagataway, or La Crosse. As the players gathered outside the fort, Lieutenant Leslye, Captain Etherington and most of the soldiers, moved outside the open gates to watch. Along the walls, blanket-draped Indian women stood.

The teams took up their positions, stripped to breechclouts and moccasins. They carried no weapons, only the webbed sticks for handling the ball. Soon the game began, both teams surging back and forth across the field in a yelling scramble of painted bodies and waving eagle plumes. Suddenly, the ball sailed up and up, then, apparently out of control, landed near the open gates.

Alexander Henry sat in his house writing letters. Hearing the shouts, he glanced out of the window. To his horror he saw that the braves had thrown down their sticks and were carrying muskets, knives, and tomahawks snatched from beneath the blankets of the waiting women.

Etherington and Leslye were overpowered and dragged off. For a few terrible moments, Lieutenent Jamet fought off the attackers with his sword. Then he went down beneath flashing tomahawks. The remaining troops tried to form into line but were cut down and scalped.

Desperate, Henry dashed to the house of his neighbor, Charles de Langlade. The Frenchman, Indian-raised, had taken part in many Indian raids against the English. Now he and his family sat calmly, watching the massacre. Henry's pleas for help fell on deaf ears. Finally a *pani* woman, or slave, took pity on him and hid the frightened trader in the attic. All night long he lay there listening to the blood-chilling whoops of the victorious Indians, who had by then killed twenty soldiers.

In the morning, Henry was greeted by the terrifying sight of an Indian named Wenniway, standing in his doorway. Paited black from head to foot with white circles around his eyes, the warrior pulled Henry from the attic and at knife point forced him to join the pitiful band of survivors. Some were killed in front of him; some actually were roasted and eaten. Henry escaped death by a miracle and was finally ransomed by a friend, Chief Wawatam, and taken to Mackinac Island for safety. Eventually Alexander Henry became a successful trader and wrote a famous book, *Travels and Adventures of Alexander Henry.* From his eyewitness account, Francis Parkman and others wrote their histories of the massacre.

The final toll was twenty-four soldiers, Lieutenant Jamet,

and one trader killed. Etherington, Leslye, eleven soldiers and Henry, along with two other traders, were prisoners.

Before long, an angry swarm of Ottawa descended on the fort. Intent on keeping the loot to themselves, the Ojibwa had not told the Ottawa of their plan. Now the Ottawa demanded all of the captives and a share of the stolen trade goods. Outnumbered, the Ojibwa agreed. Then the Ottawa, fearing a counterattack by the British, returned the prisoners unharmed to Montreal.

At Detroit, the small band of soldiers and settlers was still holding out. Finally, Fort Niagara, still strong, sent a relief force of one hundred men down river by bateau only to have them ambushed in Lake Erie. The victorious braves rowed up and down in front of the fort in the captured bateau, yelling in triumph.

When all hope seemed to be gone, twenty-two boats, carrying 260 men, finally managed to reach the fort on July 29. Led by Captain James Dalyell, Captain James Grant, and Major Robert Rogers of Ranger fame, they were determined to punish Pontiac and his warriors.

That night the troops, led by their officers, filtered silently out of the fort and by two in the morning headed for the Ottawa village. They expected to fall on the sleeping villagers and end the siege once and for all. But they failed to take the French settlers into account. They had sent word of the coming attack. As the tiny army started to cross Parent's Creek, a volley crashed out from the darkness and struck down the leaders. Ordered on, the rest of the column found themselves facing an invisible enemy. Deadly fire sent them reeling back. This time Dalyell attempted to lead a charge and was killed. Rogers and Grant, realizing their hopeless position, managed a fighting retreat, and finally reached the fort.

Pontiac had won again. Of the original force, fifty-eight officers and men were killed or wounded. And Parent's Creek became known as Bloody Run.

This skirmish was exactly to the Indians' taste. The siege was growing tiresome. They had come to the time for hand-to-hand combat and bloodshed, which they preferred. Winter was coming and, with it, the time to head for winter hunting grounds. When the siege continued to drag on, the Hurons and Potawatomi made peace with Gladwin and deserted Pontiac to a man. Finally, even the Ottawa melted away, and some of the Ojibwa chiefs sued for peace.

In spite of his steadily diminishing forces, Pontiac still held on. Then on October 20, he was given a note from Major de Villiers, commandant of Fort Chartres in the Illinois country. The note said that peace had been officially declared between England and France. He was ordered to lift the siege.

Deserted by his tribe, with no hope now of the promised French help, Pontiac finally sent a note to Major Gladwin offering peace. Then, not waiting for a reply, he left for the Illinois country.

Gaunt with hunger, the weary surviviors at last saw the fort gates swing open. The siege was over.

The following August, Colonel John Bradstreet headed for Detroit with a force of twelve hundred men. His orders were to contact the tribes, make peace, or destroy them. Weary of the long battle, the chiefs agreed to peace at last. And in July, Pontiac himself took the long journey to Fort Ontario at Oswego, New York, to surrender to Sir William Johnson. Sir William, who understood the Indian and his ways, welcomed him. After a parley, Pontiac and other western chiefs agreed to surrender and to deliver all captives. They also swore allegiance to King George III, promising to make war on any tribes who refused the terms of the treaty.

Pardoned, Pontiac returned to the Illinois country. On April 20, 1769, he was murdered by a Peoria Indian, possibly because of a feud, possibly because of his avowed friendship for the British.

Thus died a brave leader and with him the hopes of his people to drive out the British. Now, all of Canada and all of the region east of the Mississippi, including Florida, belonged to the British Crown.

At last it seemed as though the Indian threat were removed. Now a peaceful and prosperous future appeared to await the colonists. But there were other forces at work. Whereas the French had been satisfied with a military-governed society, the British colonists were an independent lot, used to handling their own affairs in this New World. Resentments grew as British troops were garrisoned in their towns, and taxes were levied for their support. From London came other taxes; one on tea led to the famous Boston Tea Party.

Along the western Great Lakes, however, many settlers remained loyal to the British Crown. Fort Michilimackinac had been reoccupied. Detroit, too, was an important military post. At Detroit, Lieutenant Governor Henry Hamilton was in charge.

Then came the outbreak of the American Revolution. With it, the Indians struck once more, this time as British allies. Detroit became the center for the raids against the colonists that followed. In 1777, fifteen war parties of whites and Indians struck deep into Kentucky, murdering and scalping men, women, and children. Few settlements escaped the terror. In Detroit, Hamilton offered prize money for captives. He also offered money for scalps and earned the hated title of "Hamilton the Hair Buyer." At times there were as many as five hundred prisoners in Detroit. Then in 1778, Shawnee raiders captured Daniel Boone. They took him to Detroit, where they turned down an offer of £100 made by Hamilton. Instead, they took him back to their village and adopted him into their tribe. But Boone was not an easy man to hold down. Learning of plans for an attack on Boonesboro, his own home settlement, he escaped and made a run to warn the settlement.

Elsewhere in the Great Lakes, the Shawnees, Delawares (Hurons), Miamis, Ottawas, Cherokees, and Foxes raided, scalped, and burned. In vain, Congress tried to crush Detroit and Hamilton.

Then, out of Kentucky, came a tough, redheaded surveyor named George Rogers Clark. Seeking out Thomas Jefferson and others, he proposed a plan to destroy the supply centers for the raids. Most were in the Illinois country dominated by Kaskaskia on the Mississippi River, Cahokia below modern St. Louis, Prairie du Rocher north of Kaskaskia, and Vincennes on the Wabash. The key to success, he argued, would be the settlers themselves. Mostly French, he felt they would welcome an attack against the British positions.

Jefferson was impressed by the hardy woodsman and succeeded in convincing Patrick Henry and the Virgina House of Burgesses of the plan's worth. Clark was granted £1,200 and the power to raise several companies of Kentucky riflemen and to secure boats and supplies.

By June 26, 1778, Clark had enlisted only two hundred men. Undaunted, he embarked on his dangerous mission.

At the mouth of the Tennessee River, he hid his boats and set off on a killing march to Kaskaskia. In spite of unbelievable hardships, the force arrived on July 4 and true to Clark's plan, the settlement surrendered without a shot being fired.

A small detachment then headed for Cahokia and Prairie

du Rocher. Both surrendered. Moving on with great skill and tact, Rogers then not only took Vincennes, but made allies of the French and the Indians as well. Ojibwa, Foxes, Ottawas, and Miamis all met with him and agreed to a truce.

When the staggering news reached Detroit, Hamilton hastily assembled a force of 175 militiamen and Indians, and set out for Vincennes. In spite of endless portages, ruined supplies, and floods, he reached his goal in December. Again the fort surrendered, this time to the British.

Clark was 180 miles away. Between him and Vincennes was a wilderness that had become one huge lake, thanks to floods. The only logical move was to retreat. Clark decided to attack.

By February they had mustered an additional eighty men, and the march began. Sloshing through icy water, waist high, over a land where game seemed to have vanished, Clark and his brave followers finally crossed the Wabash. With rations growing short, they now faced water shoulder deep. Men grew sick and were carried by stronger companions. Holding rifles and powder high above their heads, they finally straggled onto dry ground two miles from Fort Sackville, the key to Vincennes. Now, short of ammunition, with his men weak from cold and hunger, Clark sent a message to Hamilton: The Americans would capture Fort Sackville that very night! Then, in a brilliant bluff, he detailed small companies to march into Vincennes itself where they marched up and down the streets, drums beating, flags flying, in what appeared to be overwhelming numbers.

Impressed, the settlers began handing out hidden supplies of shot and powder. Before long the hardy riflemen had full bullet pouches and powder horns.

Rumors of this "powerful" army spread. Indians who had

sworn loyalty to Hamilton melted away like spring snow. Then, George Rogers Clark marched on the fort.

Fort Sackville was three acres in extent, surrounded by eleven-foot palisades topped by blockhouses. At dawn, Hamilton's guns opened fire. But Clark's forces were solidly entrenched in earthworks thrown up the night before. Instead of fleeing from the belching cannon, they calmly picked off the gunners with their long rifles. By the day's end, Hamil-

David Card

Fort Mackinac on Michigan's Mackinac Island looking toward the West Blockhouse. Round Island, in the near distance, marks the Straits of Mackinac.

ton decided he had had enough. Up went the white flag. The Illinois country at last belonged to the new United States.

Ohio and Indiana, however, were still suffering. Indians and renegade whites like the terrible Simon Girty continued to scalp, burn, and torture. Detroit still remained in British hands. And from the south, a Spanish force moved up into southern Michigan to take Fort St. Joseph.

At Fort Michilimackinac, the news of Clark's successes struck fear into the hearts of the British garrison. Deciding they could no longer defend the fort at the Straits, they decided to change their position. A few miles away, Mackinac Island seemed to be an ideal spot. The harbor was wide, and the great stone bluffs above presented an imposing position for defense. In 1780 and 1781, aided by French voyageurs, they moved cannon, buildings—everything necessary—by boat or by oxen-hauled sleds on the ice to the new fort. High on the bluff rose the "Gibraltar of the Lakes," Fort Mackinac.

Clark never attacked. Instead he won a sweeping victory over the Shawnees in the west in 1782 to end the war there. The Treaty of Paris would give the United States all of the old Northwest Territory as well as Kentucky. Thomas Jefferson and Patrick Henry had invested their money well.

In the east, however, all had not gone as well. Settlers in northeastern Pennsylvania were reeling under the blows struck by Joseph Brant and his Iroquois. By now, the Iroquois had formed themselves into a powerful confederacy, the Six Nations. Their lands reached from Lake Ontario to the Susquehanna, from the Catskills to Lake Erie. In answer to the desperate pleas of the settlers, in 1779 Washington decided that something must be done. Using troops badly needed should the British threaten from New York, he gave the orders for attack. The Iroquois country must be invaded,

Indian settlements totally destroyed, prisoners taken wherever possible.

Two expeditions set out. Both had cannon, bateau drawn by horses, herds of cattle for food. They marched with drums beating, flags flying. In spite of their clumsy size, they eventually reached the farms and homes of the Iroquois. Houses were burned to the ground, lush fields of corn, squash, beans, and pumpkins were destroyed.

Ahead of the avenging columns, the Indians and Tories were falling back. And after one failure at ambush, they continued to retreat until they reached Niagara.

With their homes and farms destroyed, the Iroquois, desperate and homeless, attempted to raid again. After the surrender of Cornwallis at Yorktown, the last of the white raiders, Walter Butler, and his Indians were finally cornered and defeated. Butler was killed, the Six Nations defeated, and America had her independence.

6

THE THIN
GRAY LINE

The year was 1812. England, fighting Napoleon, was mistress of the seas. In spite of American protests, she had been stopping American ships, claiming there were English deserters aboard. In the Northwest Territory, British and American traders met and clashed. Peaceful settlers once more listened for the sound of the war whoop. Finally, the United States declared war against England. President Madison declared that American honor must be upheld at sea, British influence over the Indians stopped, and Canada freed.

America was almost totally unprepared for war. There were only about three thousand men under arms in the American forces. These lacked formal training, and West

Point had graduated only seventy-one cadets thus far. As for experienced officers, they were as scarce as cloth to make uniforms. Early war years saw uniforms of brown, gray, or other neutral colors. Sailors' uniforms were often mistaken for British ones. Only their buttons were different, with the American showing eagle and anchor, the British an anchor only.

On the north, the American frontier was marked by Lake Huron, Lake Erie, the Niagara River, Lake Ontario, and a stretch of the St. Lawrence. Along the northern shores of Lake Ontario, Lake Erie, and the Detroit River, English settlements had sprung up. This region was known as Upper Canada and was defended by four forts—Malden, Erie, George, and Kingston. This line of forts also pointed up one of Canada's weaknesses. Settlements were in a narrow strip hugging the lakes. Once this line was cut, American forces could control everything west of it. In spite of the ill-prepared American Army and Navy, Madison decided to attack Canada.

The plan was to advance with the main army from Detroit, Niagara, and Sacket's Harbor on Lake Ontario's eastern tip. From Ohio a smaller force would move up through Michigan Territory.

This smaller force of some sixteen hundred man marched toward Detroit under General William Hull. War was officially declared on June 18, but no one thought to inform Hull of this fact. Therefore, he believed that his small schooner sailing toward Detroit was safe from the British. He put some of his sick men aboard as well as his personal papers and set out on a march overland. The British at Fort Malden were well aware of hostilities. They captured the schooner, searched her, and discovered the American plans for the attack on Canada.

By the time Hull reached Detroit, Fort Malden was protected not only by cannon, but by British war vessels standing by in Lake Erie. Hull could only wait.

Fort Mackinac on Mackinac Island was also unaware of the declaration of war. Lieutenant Hanks and his garrison of sixty-one American soldiers were completely unprepared for an attack. Even if they had known of the war, they no doubt would have expected a force to attempt a landing in the harbor. Here they were well protected by their height and their guns which commanded the Straits.

However, unknown to them, a large British force under command of Captain Charles Roberts had already landed. Instead of the fortified heights, Roberts had wisely chosen a cove on the northwest shore. The landing had taken place under cover of darkness. With Roberts was a captured island trader, Michael Dousman. From him Roberts had learned of the conditions at the fort. Roberts then sent Dousman to warn the villagers. In return Dousman agreed not to inform Hanks or the garrison.

Roberts had arrived aboard a seventy-foot armed schooner, the *Caledonia*. With him were 150 voyageurs, 280 Ottawa and Ojibwa warriors, and two six-pound cannon. At three in the morning, they started silently toward the fort a few miles away.

After the Revolution, before Mackinac was turned over to the Americans, a British officer on inspection had noticed with amazement a high unfortified bit of ground directly behind the fort. Roberts was well aware of this ridge and it was to this that he was heading. To the voyageurs, used to transporting heavy objects over rough terrain, was given the task of hauling one of the six-pounders. By dawn they had tugged and shoved the heavy piece up the steep slope. Now its muzzle pointed directly down into the sleeping fort below.

Early in the morning the fort's surgeon-mate went down to the village on an errand and came panting back to report the impending attack. Still unaware that war had been declared, Hanks called out his men. Only fifty-seven were fit. In addition their only water supply lay outside the range of the guns, making it impossible for them to withstand siege.

By the middle of the morning, the defenders could see the British grouped on the heights, the gleaming cannon's muzzle pointing directly down upon them. Beside the cannon, hordes of Indians lined the trees.

Suddenly there was a flash, a puff of smoke, and then a "boom!" Shortly after, a white flag began moving down from the heights. With it came an order to surrender in order to prevent "an effusion of blood," which would certainly follow an attack by His Britannic Majesty's forces.

Hanks had little choice. Above him waited the cannon and massacre at the hands of the already impatient Indians. Outnumbered ten to one, he surrendered.

Terms of the treaty were agreed to at noon. They generously offered to give safe conduct to all who wished to return to American territory. Any who desired could swear allegiance to the Crown and remain. Britain had won the first battle of the war.

On August 3, Lieutenant Hanks reached Detroit. Hull was dismayed at the news of the loss and at the knowledge that a horde of Indians was poised for attack. He proposed they abandon Detroit, and move into open ground where they could retreat if necessary. His Ohio militia refused to budge. In a last desperate move, Hull ordered 350 men to the Raisin River thirty-six miles south to bring back supplies.

Two days later one of the outstanding officers of the British Army, General Brock, crossed the Detroit River with 330 regulars, four hundred militia, and five cannon. To the south the brilliant war chief, Tecumseh, cut off the Raisin River detachment with a force of six hundred braves.

Hull was boxed in. He still had a force of a thousand in the fort, however, and Brock's troops had only the river at their back. But, disheartened by the refusal of his men to follow earlier orders, Hull decided not to attempt a fight. Detroit surrendered.

Hull was later convicted of cowardice and sentenced to be shot. However, President Madison pardoned him.

Meanwhile, Fort Dearborn, at the present site of Chicago, had been taken and its garrison massacred.

In the first three months of this ill-planned war, three major forts had fallen to an enemy numbering a little more than a thousand men.

In the east, the already unpopular war dragged on. The new nation, not yet organized, not united, found itself at a halt.

Then in 1813 a new plan was proposed. Fort Kingston and Fort Prescott were to be captured. The Army could then advance along the St. Lawrence against Montreal.

In order to control the Great Lakes, a fleet was built on Lake Ontario. At the base, Sacket's Harbor, seven thousand men were assembled. Commander Chauncey headed the naval operations; General Dearborn was in charge of the land armies.

Dearborn set out on an expedition, captured Fort George, and then lost it. Back at Sacket's Harbor, the British attacked the remaining garrison in force. Faced by the well-trained British regulars, the American militia turned and fled. But under the able General Jacob Brown, the regulars held and finally drove back the attack with heavy British losses. The British did succeed in destroying a nearly finished ship, the barracks, and some stores.

Failure followed failure. In the west the Americans found themselves on the defensive. Finally, in order to control Lake Erie, the government ordered Captain Oliver Hazard Perry to build and command a fleet to challenge that of Captain Barclay.

By July 1813, carpenters had completed two brigs and several smaller vessels. At the head of his tiny fleet, Captain Perry set out to find the British. His flagship was the 20-gun brig, the *Lawrence.* At her masthead flew the legend, "Don't Give Up the Ship." Ahead lay Commander Barclay with two ships, the *Detroit* and *Queen Charlotte,* as well as some smaller vessels.

Sighting the British fleet, Perry issued the orders: Close with the enemy, ship against ship. The *Lawrence* led the way, and the battle was on.

Barclay's *Detroit,* with her longer guns, fired first and severely battered Perry's flagship before she could find the range with her double-shotted carronades. Even worse, the *Niagara* lagged behind, giving the *Charlottte* time to come up and join the *Detroit* in battering the approaching *Lawrence.* Under this pounding, Perry realized he must change flagships, and he had himself rowed, bearing his flag, to the *Niagara.* Ordering his smaller vessels to follow, he once more bore down on the enemy.

This time his carronades wrought havoc. Badly wounded, the *Detroit* became fouled with the *Charlotte.* By this time the American vessels *Ariel, Scorpion,* and *Caledonia* came up. The battle raged for three hours before the British finally surrendered.

When it was over, Perry sent his now-famous message to General Harrison: "We have met the enemy and they are ours!"

With Perry's victory, the entire face of the western war was changed.

When the news of the American victory reached the British general, Procter, he ordered a retreat from Fort Malden. On October 5, General Harrison and a force of six thousand men, including regulars and Kentucky volunteers, both afoot and mounted, took off in pursuit. They met at the River Thames, and Procter, desperate, formed his infantry into a line across the road. The river protected his left flank, Tecumseh and his Indians the right. In a brilliant action, part of the Kentucky cavalry charged right through the line while the rest dismounted and drove Tecumseh's Indians into the main body of troops. Procter fled with a handful of survivors. Tecumseh was killed. The Michigan Territory was retaken.

Then in April of 1814, Napoleon abdicated the throne of France. Now England, freed from the French war, launched new expeditions against the United States. General Prevost first attempted to cut off the New England states by way of Lake Champlain. Supplies were carried by ships which had the misfortune to run into Captain Thomas Macdonough and his American fleet. In a stunning victory, Macdonough destroyed the advancing British ships. At the same time, at Plattsburg, General Alexander Macomb roundly defeated Prevost's forces. Deprived of his naval support, Prevost retreated into Canada.

A second British force captured Washington and put the Capitol, the President's Mansion, and other public buildings to the torch. But a British fleet, bombarding Fort McHenry, was beaten off. Aboard one of the vessels was an American captive, Francis Scott Key. It was here that he wrote "The Star Spangled Banner."

The final expedition was against New Orleans. Commanded by General Pakenham, a huge force of over ten thousand British, veterans of the Napoleonic Wars, sailed up the Mississippi aboard warships and transports. Opposing them were frontiersmen, deadly marksmen, as well as eight hundred regulars and the pirates of Jean Laffite. In command was General Andrew Jackson himself.

Pakenham, with his battle-seasoned veterans, had little regard for the rough frontiersmen behind their breastworks. On January 8, 1815, he ordered a full-scale attack. Line after line of redcoats surged toward the American position, only to be cut down by cannon and the long rifles of the buckskinned frontiersmen. At the end of the battle, the British had lost more than two thousand of their best fighters. American losses were only seventy.

Strangely enough, the Battle of New Orleans was fought two weeks after the peace had been signed. However, the news of this resounding defeat did much to erase the feeling of failure resulting from the earlier stages of the war.

This was the last time that American and Briton were to clash in bloody conflict. And Canada and the United States have lived as peaceful neighbors ever since.

7

CANOES AND
CARGO SHIPS

Ever since the first small bands of prehistoric Indians crossed the Bering Straits on land and by boat, the Great Lakes and the rivers that flow into them have given man freedom to travel long distances. The first dugout canoes, the swift birchbark canoes, the French bateaux—all have glided along swift rivers and the long shorelines of the Lakes. With the building of the *Griffin* and the introduction of sailboats La Salle began a new era in transportation. This era of sail was to last for nearly two hundred years.

Travel by water was filled with danger. Icy Lake Superior, shallow Lake Erie, and whitecapped Lake Michigan were all subject to sudden storms. Currents and high winds

at the Straits of Mackinac often brought sudden death to canoe and bateau alike. Rocks and rapids in the rivers called for great skill in navigation to avoid sudden disaster. The falls at Niagara were completely impassable and had to be portaged. And yet a French habitant in early Detroit would launch his canoe and head for far Quebec without a second thought for the dangers of the trip.

These water routes gave the French control over their wide western empire, while the British were blocked off on the eastern coast.

The second sailing vessel to be launched after the ill-fated *Griffin* was the forty-three-foot sloop, the *Oswego*. Built by the British on Lake Ontario in 1755, for use in the coming war, she carried twelve cannon and five swivel guns. In the following two summers, three other vessels were built—the *London, Ontario,* and *Halifax.*

At Fort Frontenac, the French were also building war ships. In June, 1756, the first naval battle of the Great Lakes took place. Three English vessels met two French ships. On the opening salvo, the British captain found himself outgunned and fled.

In 1759 mighty Fort Niagara was captured by a British force of 2300 men traveling in bateaux, whaleboats, and canoes. They also captured two French warships, the *Iroquois* and *Ouaouaise.*

At the end of the French and Indian War, the victorious British opened a shipyard at Navy Island above Niagara Falls. The first two vessels built on the Upper Lakes were the *Michigan* and *Huron.* During Pontiac's rebellion, both helped save Detroit by bringing supplies to the besieged garrison.

Between 1763 and 1812, twenty-eight more British vessels were built on Lake Ontario. The largest was the 510-ton

Niagara. A favorite name among shipbuilders, another *Niagara* was built at Erie, Pennsylvania, for Captain Perry along with his flagship, the *Lawrence.* Other vessels included a schooner and gunboat for America's first Great Lakes Navy. These vessels were hauled by oxen up to Lake Erie to join Perry.

In the final battle, Perry's victorious fleet was made up of nine ships manned by four hundred men. Barclay's forces had six vessels with heavier firepower and crewed by fifty more men.

Perry's gallant *Niagara* was raised and restored in 1913 and serves as a monument to him at Erie, Pennsylvania.

In 1818 travel on the Great Lakes improved with the building of the *Walk-in-the-Water.* The first steamship on Lake Erie, she was the third built on the Great Lakes. A cross between a steamship and sailing craft, she carried twin masts and sails to take advantage of favorable winds. Between them was a tall smokestack and high paddle wheels on either side. Her length was 132 feet, and on her first voyage from Black Rock, New York, to Detroit, crowds gathered on the shore to watch her pass. She arrived in Detroit forty-four hours after departure. At the sight of her stack belching black smoke, a French settler is supposed to have said that her power came from the "lower regions." With no sails in sight the Indians believed her to be pulled by a giant sturgeon. This was a fitting description, for her captain's name was Job Fish.

Old Fort Niagara Association

Old Fort Niagara, built circa 1725, was enlarged by Capitaine Pouchot in 1756–57. The gate was named Gate of the Six Nations, in honor of the Iroquois Confederacy.

In order to build her, the owners had ordered her engine made in New York City. From there it was hauled aboard sloops to Albany, then pulled in wagons behind three or four teams of horses to Buffalo for installation.

For the first time, passengers could make the trip to Detroit in a day and a half. Fares were $18 per person for a cabin, $7 per person for steerage.

In 1819 the *Walk-in-the-Water* headed north for Mackinac Island. There she was met at the docks by officials from the fort and the village. To celebrate her arrival, she made a short trip out into the Straits. Officials and their ladies danced on the afterdeck. Forward, the Indians held ceremonies of their own. Then in 1821, during a severe storm on Lake Erie, she struck a sandbar twelve miles out of Buffalo and was destroyed. All passengers were saved as well as the engine.

In 1822 the new steamer *Superior,* powered by the salvaged engine, and the *Henry Clay* made the Buffalo-to-Detroit run. By now, both Americans and Canadians up and down the Lakes were turning out both steam and sailing vessels. In 1835, 225 sailing ships put into Chicago's harbor.

There were many types of sailing vessels—romantic square-riggers, brigantines, schooners with two or three masts. Like their salt-water cousins, fresh-water sailors had their songs, or chanteys. They also had their special pride and their races. One chantey tells of the "Cruise of the *Bigler.*" Sailing from Buffalo to Milwaukee, she seems to have been a jinx ship. Not only was she slow, "plowing Lake Michigan," but she ran aground, broke her tug's towline, and finally smashed broadside into another ship. One line of the song says, "We could have passed the whole durn fleet if they'd stood by to wait."

Other songs were far from humorous. "Beaver Island

Boys" tells of the small ship *Lookout,* which went down with all hands off Beaver Island in northern Lake Michigan.

Up until 1841, all the Lakes steamers were side-wheelers. In that year a new type of steamship appeared. It had a screw propeller replacing the churning wheels. This propeller was attached to a long shaft which projected from the stern. As it turned, it drove the vessel through the water.

This same year, thousands of immigrants began arriving from Europe. Soon, faster ships were needed to carry these new citizens into their New World. By 1856 there were 120 steamers, 118 propeller-driven boats, and 1,149 sailing ships on the Lakes.

Up to this time, the main cargoes had been furs, grain, and freight. Now passengers became an important cargo. Several thousand settlers were heading west to the frontiers of Ohio, Illinois, Indiana, Michigan, and Wisconsin. In Michigan alone the population rose from 31,000 in 1830 to 591,000 in the 1850's. Until 1825, when the Erie Canal was finished, settlers had come overland by wagon to Buffalo, and from there boarded lake ships. The completion of this canal opened a whole new transportation era. It was started on July 4, 1817, and seemed to be an impossible task. Ohio and Indiana were not interested in the project, so New York decided to go it alone. By 1819 a fifteen-mile strip was opened from Utica to Rome, New York. Four years later the canal reached from Utica to Rochester and connected with the Hudson. In 1825, boats could travel clear from Buffalo to New York City. A favorite song of the "canawlers" was:

> I've got a mule by the name of Sal
> Fifteen miles on the Erie Canal.

Celebrations had been held as link after link was completed. The final link saw the canal boat *Seneca Chief,* with

Governor Clinton and other officials aboard, head for New York Bay. For ten days they were greeted with cheers, whistles, horns, bells, even cannon, as they traveled. The celebration was described as one honoring a nation's victory. On November 4, the boat reached the bay. Governor Clinton then poured a cask of lake water into the sea. With fireworks and boat whistles, the marriage of lake and sea symbolized a new day for Great Lakes shipping.

Before the canal, it had cost $100 to move a ton of freight from Buffalo to New York in twenty days. The canal carried the same freight in eight days for $10.

The canal was 362 miles long, four feet deep, twenty-eight feet wide at the bottom, forty feet wide at the surface. The cost was $8,000,000, a tremendous sum for those days. But traffic was so great that the cost was paid off by 1837.

Traffic was made up of passengers and freight. Passengers could choose either the packet or line boat. The packet was luxury itself, pulled by fast horses, and cost two cents a mile more than the line boat. The line boat moved more slowly, about two miles an hour, but travel was still far more pleasant than aboard a jolting wagon overland.

At Buffalo, settlers boarded lake schooners and steamers for the upper lakes. Among the steamers were the *Empire State, Michigan,* and *Northern Indiana.*

By midcentury, railroads began to replace the ships as a faster and safer means of travel. Finally, passenger ships were scrapped or turned into cargo vessels.

In 1855 iron ore was discovered in Michigan's Upper Peninsula. Although the cheapest way to handle it was at mills on the lower Lakes, the old problem still remained. It was the same one that had vexed the early voyageurs. Where the St. Mary's River connected Lake Superior and Lake

Huron, the water dropped a full eighteen feet. At first, some vessels were built below Lake Superior and then dragged overland for launching, on rollers. The first ship to make the crossing this way was the schooner *Algonquin* in 1840. Five years later the steam-propeller ship *Independence* crossed with the *Julia Palmer,* a side-wheeler. By 1846 there were still only twelve vessels on Lake Superior. In order to develop this rich mining region, improved transportation methods had to be found. The tramway with horsedrawn cars to carry cargo around the rapids was no longer efficient enough. The answer would have to be a canal.

Congress listened to the case, then decided in the words of Henry Clay that it was a "work quite beyond the remotest settlement of the United States if not on the moon." Finally in 1852 an act was passed giving Michigan 750,000 acres of public land and a right-of-way. The money from the sale of land would be used to pay for the building of a canal.

At the Sault, recovering from typhoid fever, was a remarkable young man named Charles T. Harvey. He was the western agent for the Fairbanks Scale Company of Vermont. Traveling through Michigan's Upper Peninsula he, too, soon realized that great wealth lay in the mines waiting to be taken out and down the Lakes, and he was sure a canal could be built to do the job.

The Fairbanks Scale Company had faith in Harvey and agreed to undertake the project if Harvey could convince the Michigan Legislature. Harvey went to work. His plans were sound, his reasoning sure. A Michigan act was passed in 1853 authorizing the payment of 750,000 acres of land of their choice to any company willing to undertake the building of the canal.

Fairbanks accepted the contract. Harvey was appointed

general agent in charge. Captain Augustus Canfield, U.S. Topographical Engineers, was appointed by the governor as chief engineer.

In April, Harvey went down to Detroit. Here he bought horses, tools, and supplies, and hired workmen. Back at the Sault, he rented the Indian Agency building as headquarters, built a hospital, bunkhouses, and mess halls.

On June 4, work commenced. It soon became clear that the project would be harder than anyone had imagined. Captain Canfield died and was replaced by other engineers but the burden fell directly on Harvey's shoulders. Beneath the surface the workers struck solid rock. Impatient at the slow work with pick and shovel, Harvey designed and built his famous "Harvey's Hammer." A forged-steel pointed cylinder, it was lifted, then dropped, over and over again to break out the rock. But more trouble awaited him. Winter temperatures plummeted to 30 degrees below zero. In 1854, the dread plague, cholera, swept the settlement. Many died. At times as many as sixteen hundred men were needed on the job. But few wanted to work in the bitter cold, shut off from civilization for months at a time. So immigrants landing in New York were recruited for work at the Sault.

In spite of these overwhelming odds, just a short while before the two-year contract was to expire, Harvey completed the canal. It was 5400 feet long, 100 feet wide. Two locks each 350 feet long and 70 feet wide would raise or lower vessels the eighteen feet between the lakes. The cost was nearly a million dollars. As payment for this cost, Harvey and others from the Ship Canal Company chose top timber and mineral lands as agreed.

The shippers also got their money's worth. Shipment of iron ore jumped eight times in volume. Copper shipments

The Sault Sainte Marie Locks, circa 1890. Here the steamer North West *is being lowered in the newly enlarged locks for her trip into the lower Great Lakes.*

doubled. Toll charges began whittling away at operation cost. In the first year $4,374 was collected. In 1860 tolls brought in $24,660.

A vessel bound for Lake Superior first entered the lower lock. Gates, with a long boom and cable attached, were closed behind by men turning a capstan. Valves were then opened in the upper gates allowing water to enter and raise the ship to the level of the upper lock. The dividing gates were then opened, and the vessel floated through. Now the upper gates were closed, water again admitted, and when the water level of Lake Superior was reached, the ship floated out. For the return to Lake Huron, the process was reversed.

Thousands of tons of freight began passing through. Copper, iron ore, and wheat went down the Lakes; lumber and coal came up.

In 1881, ownership of the canal was turned over to the United States Government. The locks were enlarged, tolls were removed, and passage is still free today.

In 1913 another important canal was built. This Welland Canal bypassed Niagara Falls, lowering ships a full 327 feet into Lake Ontario. The portages of the voyageurs were now a thing of the past.

Lake vessels, too, were changing. By 1873 there were fifteen hundred sailing ships on the Lakes. During the great lumber era, schooners carried their cargoes of lumber down to the Lakes to rebuild Chicago after the terrible Chicago fire and to build houses and buildings across half the nation.

Colorful as they were, sailing vessels were slow, and they had to depend upon favorable winds to move. Tugboats towed lines of schooners through the rivers but towed vessels were difficult to maneuver in narrow channels. Because of their small size, they were unable to carry large ore shipments. By 1900 only eight hundred schooners remained.

Improvements were also called for in ore handling. In the beginning, men loaded the ore by hand, carried it in wheelbarrows onto the dock and dumped it into the ship's hold. For unloading, the crew shoveled the ore out by hand and dumped it in buckets, which were hoisted out and dumped on shore.

Curran Russell Collection

A *Great Lakes schooner, the* Sidney O. Neff, *is towed into port by a steam tug amid heavy seas. Often several schooners were hauled at once in a long line by the powerful tugs.*

"Red Iron Ore," a lake chantey of the time, tells of the disgusted sailors who felt it beneath their calling to load and unload the dirty red ore.

Gradually, machinery replaced this slow and backbreaking chore. To carry the ore a new type of vessel appeared. Her shape would influence the building of all lake vessels to come. The *R. J. Hackett*, wooden hulled, had her control bridge moved far forward, and her machinery housed far back at the stern. The long waist of the ship held hatches. Into these the red ore poured down from loading docks. On the docks high trestles bore loaded ore cars which dumped the ore into bins. The bins were then opened, and the ore ran down into the open hatches and into the hold. Three or four ships could be loaded at one time.

During the 1860's, steel-hulled vessels, which could be built far longer than wooden vessels, appeared on the Lakes. The first was the 287-foot *Onoko.*

One of the strangest vessels of all was the iron whaleback. Built with a rounded topside, she looked like a floating cigar or surfaced submarine. These were later replaced by longer ships over seven hundred feet long capable of carrying twenty thousand tons of ore.

Today, there are many types of vessels on the Lakes. There are bulk carriers of ore, grain, and coal. There are package freighters, oil tankers; self-unloaders for transporting stone, coal, and cement. There are railroad ferries, canal boats, fishing vessels, automobile ferries, passenger boats, and pleasure craft.

The building of the St. Lawrence Seaway has brought further changes to the Lakes. Following the route of the old fur traders, it was constructed by Canada and the United States and connects the Lakes with the Atlantic Ocean in a manner that Governor Clinton never dreamed possible.

One of the great engineering feats of our time, it enables
"salties,"—salt-water ships from all over the world—to touch
at major lake ports. Vessels from other lands now have a
lake coast of 8,300 miles, longer than the entire American
Atlantic coast, to visit. Many Great Lakes ports have become
seaports as well.

This is the story of Great Lakes shipping. It is one that
ranges from canoes to cargo ships in a little more than four
hundred years.

8

WITH CALLOUSED HANDS

After the glaciers came the forests. Following the forests, the animals, the Indians, and finally the settlers from the Old World. Slowly then, for the first time, the forest edge began to be pushed westward. Trees were girdled and burned to clear the fields for farming. Others were felled for fuel or logs to build homes, barns, and forts. Along the eastern Great Lakes, soaring pines, bearing the brand of the King's broad arrow, became tall masts for the Royal Navy.

After the American Revolution, settlements grew as the pioneers moved deeper and deeper into the wilderness. Soon, early sawmills were cutting logs into boards. Boards meant houses and barns, churches, schools, and ships. For more

than three hundred years, wood furnished the building blocks of a new nation.

To supply this growing demand, logging began its march from New England. Logging is the felling of trees, the cutting of trunks into logs, and the transporting of logs to the cutting mill.

As early as 1623, New England's timberlands rang with the sounds of axes, the cries of ox drivers. The best wood for general use came from the white pine which at first seemed to be limitless. As the pine ran out in New England, loggers moved on west. By 1840, New York was the prime log producer. In 1860 Pennsylvania held the record. Ten years later, Michigan was king. But by 1900, Wisconsin held the world record for white pine logged to the mills.

This "limitless" forest of over 800 million acres had been the finest timber resource in the world. By 1900, one third of it was destroyed. In spite of the thoughtless cutting and the waste in slashings, which often flamed up to destroy entire towns, this era was one of the most colorful in Great Lakes' history.

Logging followed a familiar pattern. Winter was the time for cutting. Not only did snow and ice provide sled transportation, but farmers could go to the woods for winter work. Spring meant swollen rivers, transportation for the millions of logs heading to the mills.

The first man to go into the woods was the "land looker," or timber cruiser, hired by the lumber companies. An expert in judging both timber quality and transportation possibilities, he scouted the great stands of pine alone. Carrying only the simplest camping equipment, he checked boundaries, marked his findings in forty-acre tracts, and moved on.

Behind him came the carpenters, the blacksmith, the horses, and the road builders. Camps were set up near the

F. M. Longyear Collection

In 1886 frontier towns like this were being carved out of the wilderness. Rough lumber houses sprang up beside the stumps fronting the muddy main street.

cutting areas. These had bunkhouses, a cook and mess shack, a barn, and a company store. All were rough, mud-caulked logs. All were temporary. Oxen were used first, then the horse. Meanwhile the "road monkeys" were cutting the main road. This road was for hauling and had to be made level with piled brush or dirt so that the huge sleighs would be able to pass safely. Leading to this road were hauling roads coming out from cutting areas. Down the road from town, the "tote-road," came the teamster with a huge load of supplies for hungry men. Tea, coffee, sugar, flour by the barrelful, dried fruit, salt pork. Behind him came the crew, each carrying his gear, called his "turkey."

Each member of the crew had his specialty, from the "chickadees" who cleaned the roads, to the skilled teamsters and "top-loaders." Also expert were the axemen. They could drive a stake for a target and fell a tall tree directly on it.

At first, only axes were used. Some were double-bitted, sharp on both sides. With the invention of the two-handed crosscut saw, both axes and saws were used. To fell a forest giant, the men worked in pairs. Axes cut the notch, or "scarf"; the long saws finished the cut. As the great pine trembled, the saw was pulled clear and with the shout of "Timber!" all scattered to watch the tree crash down to an earth-shaking thud. Then swampers began lopping off branches and sawing the tree into logs.

Next, held by huge steel tongs, the logs were "snaked" out behind a team to the main road. There they were piled in a "skid" to await the heavy sleigh.

Meanwhile, nightly visits by the "icer" had turned the road into a long skating rink. These icers were sleds carrying boxes filled with water. The water sprayed out onto the surface and froze, leaving a slick surface with cut-in ruts or tracks to guide the sleigh runners. Over this route, teams

Some of the Wisconsin shanty boys are standing above a prize load of logs, weighing about 100,000 pounds, in 1892. Note the ravaged land in the background.

could haul unbelievably large loads. The largest ever hauled on sleds by horses weighed 250 tons! Hauled fifteen miles by six horses, it held enough logs to fill nine railroad flatcars.

To load these sleighs called for skill and daring. Here the "top-loaders" waited on top of the growing pile. Chains, pulled by a horse, dragged each log up steep bunks to the top. Then in a split second the loaders had to guide the heavy log into place and leap aside. Failure to judge the distance could result in smashed legs or worse. When the load limit was reached, all logs were secured with heavy chains. The teamster mounted the huge pile, spoke to his team, and moved out.

To handle the clumsy logs, the loggers or "shanty boys," used an unusual tool, called a peavey after its inventor. The handle, about two baseball bats long, was stout and steel-tipped; it carried a steel hook swinging from an iron band. This hook could close tightly around a log. As the iron tip held, the heavy handle became a powerful lever.

When the load of logs reached the river bank, it was piled high on the rollway to await the spring thaw.

Day after day the work went on. The work week was six days long. It began before sunup and ended after dark. Breakfast was signaled by an ear-splitting sound from a struck iron triangle or by a horn. Food was plain but plentiful. Talking was forbidden at table, and the cook was top boss. Noon meals were sledded out to the men at the cutting stands. Dinner was late, plentiful, and also silent. Then lights out and snoring men in lines of bunks, until once more the "gut-hammer" signaled a new day.

With Sundays off, Saturday night was the time for recreation. Tale tellers sat on a bench called the "deacon's seat." A fiddle, guitar, or mouth organ would accompany favorite songs. The "Jam on Gerry's Rock" told the sad tale of the drowning of Young Monroe. "The Little Brown Bulls" recounted the stirring contest between the Scotsman's big spotted steers and the Yankee's little brown bulls. The bulls won. Other songs told of fights, sad love affairs, or river tragedies. Many began with the phrase, "Come all ye . . . ," a line borrowed from earlier Irish ballads.

With the first signs of spring, most of the men were paid off and the horses sent home before thaw. Now came the time of the "river-hogs." These were young men, daring, quick, "catty" of foot. To help them ride the rearing, plunging, rolling logs, they wore boots with spiked soles. In their hands they held peaveys or the longer cant hooks. Pay was higher. There were many graves along the river routes to remind them of the danger.

If the logs were white pine, they could be floated down log by log. Hardwoods had to be made into rafts with lighter woods beneath to buoy them up.

First the rollways had to be broken out. Skilled rivermen searched for the key log that held the pile. Finding it, they twisted the log free, then leaped for their lives. Behind them the huge mass grumbled, moved, then came careening down into the flood below with a tremendous splash. Before long, the entire river was a solid mass of hurrying logs.

Now the rivermen moved tirelessly. Some followed on shore, others rode the logs themselves, prying, lifting, keeping the drive moving. A slip or misstep could mean a crushing death. Night and day, wet to the armpits, they worked. Behind them floated the "wanigan" or floating supply boat. Aboard were food, supplies, and rough bunks for exhausted rivermen.

Log jams were the most dangerous of all happenings on

the river. Rapids, river bends, gorges—all could catch and hold a log while hundreds piled up behind it in minutes. These jams had to be broken at all costs. Sometimes a key log could loosen the mounting jumble of the big "sticks"; other times, dynamite had to be used. Once the jam broke, the river-hogs had to scramble for safety across the sea of logs or be crushed.

Eventually, the drive reached the long journey's end. Now, millions of logs, each bearing the hammered-on log mark of the owners, were sorted into the log corrals or "booms." Sorters stood by watching for special marks such as the Flying M, the Hanging Man, the Circle Q. From the booms the logs traveled up the conveyors into the mill where the highly skilled sawyers sawed them into boards on the singing circular saws. Timber was then loaded aboard schooners, steamers, or railroads, for markets across the country.

Felling and hauling, the loggers kept on winter after winter. At last, the rich forests had become raw stumps lined with the piles of brush slashings.

Then one day, the white pine was gone from the Great Lakes, and the loggers moved on to the yellow pine, the Douglas fir, the redwoods of the west.

This ravaging of the forests taught a bitter lesson. Today, replanting, better fire prevention, water and soil conservation promise new forests for future generations.

If pine provided riches above ground, minerals offered wealth beneath. Typical of early mining methods were those used in the Upper Peninsula of Michigan. Here in the land of the Old Copper Culture Indians lay hidden wealth within the nation's boundaries—boundaries set by treaty after the Revolution.

This early drawing portrays one of the first copper mines at the tip of Michigan's Upper Peninsula.

Copper was found and used first. Then in 1841, iron ore was discovered. Prospectors flooded in. But it wasn't until 1845 that copper mining began in earnest with the Cliff Mine, which gave up forty million pounds before it ran out.

Other mines were opened, and with the building of the Sault Canal, transportation for the ore became far easier. Iron mines also found it profitable to ship ore to the lower Lakes.

In the beginning, mines were merely large open holes or pits. As digging continued, mines were forced to go deeper into "shafts." These were deep reinforced holes leading down into the earth.

Like logging, mining was dangerous work. And unlike the logger, the miner had only his hat-mounted candle for light. The sun, the snow, the blue sky—these were not for him.

Methods were crude. Holes for explosives were made by hand. One man held an iron bar, while others drove it into the rock with sledges. Into the holes went the gunpowder. After the blast, shattered rock had to be crushed by men with hammers.

As the broken rock was brought up, the shafts grew deeper. These shafts not only carried the miners up and down in "cages" supported by cables, but held "skips," or buckets, for raising the ore to the surface. Deep in the dark shaft, tunnels reached out in crosscuts, or "drifts." Finally even the drifts had smaller shafts, or "rises," leading from one drift to another.

At first ore was shoveled into cars and hauled to the lifting skip. Later, ore was allowed to drop down one of the rises into a waiting car.

Many of the foremen were experienced miners from Cornwall, England. These Cornishmen carried a special kind of food into the mines. Called a pasty (pāhstee), it was a dough pancake filled with meat and vegetables. Heated on a miner's shovel over a candle, it made a hot and delicious midday meal.

Between 1870 and 1900, modern methods began to appear in mining operations. Engines replaced horses and mules for hauling ore cars. Electric motors pumped water from the shafts; electric lights replaced the flickering candles. Mechanical crushers broke up the rock; dynamite replaced gunpowder.

For many years, Michigan's Upper Peninsula, northern Wisconsin, and eastern Minnesota led the world in iron ore production. And Lake Superior carried the ore to the busy furnaces on the lower Lakes.

Most of these great mines are no more. But modern treating of poorer-grade ore may bring them back to life once again.

Until the Civil War, the Great Lakes area was mainly engaged in farming. Mills ground grain; small sawmills turned out lumber. By 1860, however, for the first time industry pushed ahead of agriculture in production. War, as always, had caused a speedup in manufacturing, and industry grew rapidly. Increased population also created a greater demand for manufactured goods. Meanwhile on the Lakes, a new industry had sprung up—commercial fishing.

Until 1800, the tremendous numbers of fish in the Lakes had hardly been touched by the Indians. There were many species, such as the giant sturgeon, tasty whitefish, lake trout often running up to ninety pounds. In addition there were yellow pike, lake herring, chubs and great schools of tiny smelt. And smoked whitefish, herring, and chubs are still real delicacies.

Early fishermen had plenty of pine and oak with which to build their own sailing boats. One type of fishing vessel, the Mackinaw Boat, was the only one of its kind in the world. Originally designed by the French, it was pointed at the bow and flat-bottomed. Later it became pointed at both ends with a single stout mast forward. Ropes, or shrouds, leading from the mast to the gunwales for support, were omitted for easier net handling.

To build a fishing boat, oak was sawed and hewn with axes into large "knees," or braces, beams, and planks. Oak "ribs" were made with great care; all wood was carefully dried and seasoned. Then the bottom beam or "keel" was laid and the oak ribs attached. Over this skeleton, oak planks were bent and fastened with wooden pegs driven into auger-bored holes. Next the pine mast was "stepped" or set up and the deck built across the top with an open waist for crew and cargo. Canvas sails and supporting lines were added. Oars were carried for calm, windless weather, as well as for easier maneuvering when setting nets.

At first, fresh-water fish was eaten only by those living near the Lakes. With the coming of improved eastward transportation, fishermen began sending their catches to a new market. To preserve them, some fish were smoked, and others were packed in ice in barrels, some were salted.

Fishing ports sprang up along the coasts. Docks held shanties for gear and cross-armed frames for drying nets. Some fish were taken with hook and line. One type of gear was made up of rows of hooks hanging baited from a long float line held up by cork floats. These baited lines were coiled in tubs before use. Great skill was needed to pay out the line without snarling it or snagging fingers.

Like cargo vessels, sail finally gave way to steam and then

In 1890 the Indians were still fishing in the swift and dangerous rapids of Ste. Marie's River. These rapids had long blocked entrance into Lake Superior by large vessels and made the building of the Sault Sainte Marie Canal a necessity.

to motor-powered boats or "tugs." High-sided for rough weather, most were small and without crew's quarters like those on salt-water craft. Distances were shorter on the Lakes and most fishermen made port every night.

Fishing methods improved with the boats. Pound nets were set for trapping fish, gill nets entangled fish in the mesh, and finally, trawls scooped up the fish.

However, 1940 saw the peak of commercial fishing on the Lakes. Over-fishing, water pollution, and the coming of the sea lamprey caused a steady decline in the industry.

These lampreys possess round sucking mouths with sharp needlelike teeth inside. They attach themselves to other fish, puncture their flesh, then suck out their life blood. How the lamprey, a salt-water creature, ever entered the Lakes is something of a mystery. One dwarf type lived in Lake Ontario for many years but was kept from spreading by the falls of the Niagara River. Perhaps the lampreys attached themselves to the bottoms of vessels passing up the Welland Canal. In any event, they spread into the fishing grounds and began their deadly work.

Today, chemicals and river barriers are winning the fight against these marauders. Perhaps with wise fish planting, conservation, and pollution control, the fishing industry on the Lakes may be revived.

These three industries are only a few of those which have used the natural resources of the Great Lakes. All have their special skills; all brought in workers not only from the East but from other nations as well. Many carried on the work of their fathers. Dutch, Irish, Finns—all seafaring people— found fishing to their liking. Germans, Scandinavians, and French preferred the woods. The English, the Poles, and others preferred the familiar mines. Some gathered in the industrial centers. But all shared their skills, their customs, and their folklore. And they gave us a rich heritage of men of all races and colors, men with calloused hands and brave hearts. The men who helped carve a civilization out of a wilderness.

9

TALL MEN AND
TALL TALES

Everyone likes to hear a good tale told well. From the beginning of man, all peoples of all colors have had their folk tales and tellers of tales. These stories handed down by word of mouth through countless generations may change slightly with the times. But all contain something special that makes them live on.

In the world of unwritten folklore, there are tales of giants and dwarfs, of tricksters, animals who behave like people, heroes, demons, poor boys who make good. Most are told for two reasons. One is to explain the unknown to primitive peoples, such as the birth of the earth, the stars, the movements of sun and moon, the coming of seasons and storms.

112

A second is the explanation of the customs of a people, a sort of spoken textbook for the young, so that they may learn the ways of their special culture.

The Great Lakes region has its own special tales, beginning first with the Indian legends, then tales brought from Europe, and finally American folklore—backwoods and pioneer stories, stories of boasters, fighters, bad men, humorous liars, heroes.

The American Indian divided his legends into two types. One dealt with the distant past and of things no longer possible. The second group told of the everyday world. Among the Winnebagos of Wisconsin, the first type was considered sacred; the second consisted of legends to be told again. Sacred tales could not be told in summer when the snakes were above ground. Nor could the hero die or be killed forever, for these were the immortals. The second type could be told at any time, but they must end in tragedy. Heroes were humans, or humans who could change into animals, or spirits who lived among men. But all legends were told by special people who had the magic gift of storytelling. Some of the storytellers preferred to retell tales in the exact words of the earlier tellers. Others added ideas to make them more exciting or meaningful. Acting ability was important also.

Heroes of sacred tales were Sun, Morning Star, Water Spirit, Thunderbird, or the strange foolish hero called Trickster. Animal spirits—Hare, Wolf, Bear, and Turtle—ruled the animal world. These heroes often helped man by bringing him fire, the bow and arrow, healing arts; or sometimes they destroyed evil spirits that threatened the tribe. Land forms, rocks, falls, odd formations were also created by these spirits.

One such story comes from the Senecas of New York. It begins as follows: Floating Cloud was the most beautiful of all maidens in the villages. At last the tale of her beauty reached a chief from another clan. A brave and great chief, he was not young, and he was known as Ugly One.

When Ugly One heard of Floating Cloud, he sent a runner to her father carrying many rich and beautiful gifts. Pleased at the honor, Floating Cloud's father accepted the marriage offer. The entire village was filled with excitement, for Ugly One would bring his young braves to the village.

But Floating Cloud was heartbroken. Not only was her husband old, but he was ugly. Her dream of marrying a fine young brave, arrow straight, was gone forever. In despair, she leaped into her canoe and sent it headlong toward the terrible waterfalls below the village. Better death than marriage to the Ugly One.

But the Spirit of the Harvest and Rain, who lived in a cave beneath the falls, saw her. Not wishing her to die, he caught her up in his arms just as her canoe smashed itself on the jagged rocks.

Floating Cloud dwelt in the Spirit's cave for many moons. There she learned many secrets. One was the reason for the strange sickness that had killed so many of her people. This sickness, the Spirit said, came from a giant serpent who lived beneath the village. It was this snake who poisoned the water, so that many would die and he could have much human flesh to eat.

Then one day, the Ugly One died. Floating Cloud returned to her village and told of the giant snake. The people listened and then moved closer to the lake. For a time, all was well. But finally the snake rose up and followed. Again the sickness brought wailing to the women of the Senecas. Four times the village moved; four times the serpent followed. But at the last time of his moving, the Harvest Spirit caught him in the open and struck him with a mighty thunderbolt.

Wounded, the snake flung his great body across the land, tearing up trees, crushing rocks with his thrashing coils. Again the Spirit sent a crashing thunderbolt, and again. With the fourth bolt, the terrible serpent lay dead. From head to tail he measured twenty arrow flights.

Now the tribe gathered. Men, women, and children pushed and tugged until they rolled the dead serpent into the river. As big as a mountain, he floated down until he became wedged between the rocks. Over the body rose the river, forcing the snake's body out into a giant bow. From his body the curve of Niagara Falls was formed.

This legend is typical of earth spirits and the formation of natural land shapes. Another tale, from the Ojibwa, not only explains a strange rock, but teaches a moral to the young men.

The main character is called Manibozho by the Ojibwa. He appears in the legends of other tribes as the Winnebago Trickster, the Siouxian Spider, or in the western tribes as Coyote, Raven, or Old Man.

Manibozho was old. It was now the time for sitting alone in his lodge far from man, a time for peace.

But in the Ojibwa village were ten young men. All had heard since childhood the tales of the great Manibozho and of his magic. Together they decided to seek him out and ask that each brave's wish be granted.

Four moons they traveled, up distant rivers, through silent forests. At last on the Island of the Great Turtle, they found him.

Greeting them, each asked to be allowed one wish in return for their hard journey. At last, Manibozho agreed.

The first asked to become a mighty warrior, the second a wise prophet, the third a great hunter, the fourth a maker of arrows, the fifth a tireless dancer, the sixth a strong man, the seventh a skilled canoe maker, the eighth a teller of tales, the ninth a healer. All wishes were granted. And then the tenth asked for eternal life.

Manibozho was sad. This was the one gift denied all mortals. But wishing to keep his promise, Manibozho finally spoke. "Your wish is granted," said he. Raising his medicine bundle he turned the tenth man into a towering rock. There he stands to this day, living forever but with no life.

A legend special to the Great Lakes tells why the weather is so changeable.

Two brothers, Manibozho the Good, and Peepaukawis the Bad, decided to run a foot race. Across the land they sped with Peepaukawis, the elder, in the lead. Wherever he ran, the sky darkened, storms raged, snow fell, the birds ceased their singing. Behind him Manibozho hurried on. In his moccasin prints the snow melted, flowers grew, the sun shone, and the birds and animals greeted him happily. For many moons Peepaukawis was in the lead and the ground was frozen. At last he lay down to rest. Quickly Manibozho dashed past him. For five moons he ran while the earth smiled. At last, Peepaukawis called out, "I am beaten, brother." And so, Manibozho rested. Too late, he saw that it was a trick. Peepaukawis raced past him, and once more the earth grew cold. With his last strength, the younger brother leaped up, reached his brother, and passed him.

For a short time he stayed ahead and then fell back. And now, when it is warm in late fall, the people know that Manibozho has dashed ahead, and it is Indian summer. For the rest of the year, no one knows who will win.

These legends are very much shortened. The storyteller took much longer in order to entertain and teach his listeners. Some stories are in parts. Some are rich in humor. Indians, too often, are pictured as stern and nonsmiling. Actually their sense of humor is tremendous among their own people.

Often the white man found himself the object of their jokes. One story told is said to have taken place in northern Michigan.

Winter was approaching, and it was time to cut firewood for the coming cold. The town banker had his wood already stacked, earlier than usual. A traveler asked him why. Joseph Cornplanter, he said, an Indian living across the river, had begun cutting the week before. Knowing the woods knowledge of Indians, based on the thickness of fur on the animals, the behavior of geese and other birds, the banker stated that he always watched Joe to find out the time to cut firewood.

Curious, the traveler visited Joe Cornplanter. How did he know when it was time to cut wood?

Joe spoke solemnly. Every fall, he said, the banker would sharpen his axe, stand it by the woodshed, then watch across the river. That, Joe said, was the time for him to go into the woods. Any man as smart as the town banker certainly must know when winter was coming.

Early settlers, too, had their special brand of humor, and tall tales as well.

An Indian named Fred Redbird caught a fine big northern pike one day and, having plenty of fish to eat, put the pike in his rain barrel. The pike lived, and Fred named him Charlie. Every day he fed Charlie worms or minnows, and the fish grew.

It was a dry summer, that year, and Fred finally got tired of carrying water to fill the barrel. So he decided he'd teach Charlie to live out of water. Every day he'd take Charlie out and let him lie on the wet grass for a spell. He left him in the shade for a few minutes every day. Finally the pike got so he could stay out half a day at a time. Charlie got pretty tame with all this. He even started following Fred when he went to dig worms for supper.

At the end of summer, Fred decided it was time to go to town and lay in some supplies for winter. So he took off across his rickety bridge that spanned the stream, heading for town. Charlie followed, moving sort of like a snake and just about as fast. Fred decided he'd let him come. It was good having company. He crossed the bridge, stepping over the one missing plank, and struck off through the woods.

Suddenly he remembered Charlie. Glancing back he saw the fish was missing. He turned around and hurried back thinking maybe Charlie had fallen through the missing plank. Sure enough, there in the stream beneath the bridge lay Charlie, belly up in the water. He'd fallen into the water and drowned.

Backwoods stories had their humor, and they had their heroes and giants as well. The best known are those about that mightiest of all loggers, Paul Bunyan. Among his feats was the building of the Great Lakes with the help of Babe, the Blue Ox.

Some say Paul was born in Wisconsin, some say Michigan or Minnesota. Probably he came down from New England with the first loggers. In any case he could stride over mountains or fell a whole stand of pine with one stroke of his axe.

They say Paul grew mighty fast as a youngster. His first cradle was outgrown in the first week. Paul's Pa had to stop and build a new one out of seven-foot boards. It took him a week, and by that time Paul was already eight feet long.

This time his Pa decided he'd do it right. He hitched up his oxen, took his axe, and headed into the woods. When he came back he had a twenty-five-foot log, white pine, straight as a fiddle string. Working night and day he hollowed it out using his adze and fire. But again he was too late. Paul's bare toes hung out the end, and for a while they thought he was stuck for good.

This time Paul's pa didn't try anything fancy. He had a full tree cut into boards and made him a fifty-foot box. Too big for cradle rockers, he hauled it into the St. Lawrence instead and anchored it with fourteen logging chains and a cable from a three-masted schooner. When Paul crawled in, he looked happy as a bear in a honey tree. His pa was mighty glad. He'd gone without sleep for weeks. Now with the waves rocking the cradle, he figured Paul would sleep for a while.

Paul had different ideas. He enjoyed the rocking so much he caused a tidal wave that nearly wiped out the State of New York.

Next morning, Paul was gone. He'd hoisted the cradle on one shoulder, the chains over the other, and took the cable for a belt. Heading west, he picked up a logging crew on the way and finally turned the cradle into a bunkhouse.

The stories kept turning up. Some said Paul had built himself a house so tall that the top story had to be on hinges to let the moon go by. As for feeding his crew, he had a pancake griddle so big it took four men with bacon strapped on their feet to grease it.

Then came the winter of the Blue Snow. It got so cold the men's voices froze in the air and never thawed out till spring, causing the greatest racket ever heard in the Great Lakes country. More important, Paul found a newborn ox struggling in the water and carried him home to thaw out. Blue as the snow, he took to Paul right away, and Paul named him Babe because he'd found him as a baby.

After a while Babe got so big he measured fourteen axe handles and a plug of tobacco between his horns. With this new helper, Paul not only dug the Lakes, but he hitched Babe to the crooked roads in the state and pulled every single one straight.

As for logging, Paul had a specialty. He'd pick out a stand of timber, then with four strokes, north, south, east, and west, square off each pine. When they all stood peeled and square, he'd mow them down with his axe, throw a logging chain around them, and Babe would haul them down to the water. They did this with an acre of trees at a time.

When it was time to move, the whole camp was hitched up behind Babe. Bunkhouse, store, cook shack, barns— everything would move out in a long line to the new cutting grounds.

In no time at all, the camp moved across Michigan, Wisconsin, and Minnesota.

Besides Babe, there were many strange animals in the woods at that time. To keep them straight, Paul had his clerk, Johnny Inkslinger, make a list. Here are just a few of them.

AXEHANDLE HOUND: Sometimes called Wood Muncher. A long-bodied, hatchet-headed dog whose only food was wood. He preferred axe handles and peaveys and often raided the camps to fill his hunger.

BABALORIUS: A three-tailed half bird, half beast. He had a single twisted horn growing out of his forehead; his top half was covered with feathers, lower parts half bison and half lion. One tail was barbed for hunting, one flat for fly swatting, and the third feathered for ornament and carried over his left shoulder.

BILDAD: Around lakes, the smack of the Bildad's tail on the water is often mistaken for the sound of a paddle. About the size of a large beaver, it has kangaroo hind legs, webbed feet, and a hawk's bill. Upon sighting leaping trout, its favorite food, the Bildad will leap high into the air, then smack the fish senseless with his tail on the way down. Only one shanty boy ever tried to eat a Bildad. After the first bite he leaped up, hopped to the water's edge, and with a tremendous leap bounded sixty feet to the middle of the pond and landed sitting down. He sank like a stone.

SIDEHILL LANCER: A creature living on hillsides having two short legs on the uphill side.

SPLINTER CAT: A hard-faced raccoon- and honey-eater. It leaps at tree after tree, splintering them with his hard head, hoping for food. The damage resulting from his nightly hunts is often blamed on windstorms.

These are only a few of Paul's animal acquaintances. And only a few of his adventures. There were other heroes as well. Joe Magarac, the mighty giant from the Pennsylvania steel mills, was built of steel. And there were real men whose legends spread—men like Davy Crockett, Daniel Boone, Mike Fink, Johnny Appleseed. Most came into the Great Lakes country at one time or other, cutting logs, making steel, planting orchards. They were tall men who helped shape America.

10

THE STATES
THEMSELVES

Eight states touch the Great Lakes. Each has its own history, land shape, products. Each is an interesting story in itself. Briefly, here are the eight states and their beginnings arranged alphabetically.

ILLINOIS

Admitted to the Union in 1818, this state is called the Prairie State. It lies in the heart of the Middle West. Early Indians there were called the *Illini*, meaning *men*. Called Illinois by the French, they gave the state her name.

Both Father Marquette and Jolliet claimed the area for

France in 1673. Illinois remained a part of New France until 1765 when the British took control. In 1778, George Rogers Clark claimed it for America.

As settlers moved in, the Indians resisted. In 1812 the Potawatomi chief, Metea, led them into battle. Fort Dearborn fell. Again in 1832 Black Hawk led them in a final attempt to drive out the whites. Defeated, the Indians were forced to move away.

The prairies provided rich soil, and the wide range of temperature helped produce many crops. To share in this fine farm land, settlers came from Indiana, Ohio, New England, New York, and Pennsylvania. From Europe came Irish, Poles, Italians, Germans, and others. Many settled in the teeming city of Chicago. Public schools and social workers such as Jane Addams helped them to become a part of America.

Both President Lincoln and President Grant were elected from Illinois.

Today more than half of the population lives in cities. But over twenty thousand farms still produce corn, grains, cereals, and fruit. The state ranks third in soft-coal mining. Petroleum refining supplies fuels for diesel engines across the nation. Meat packing and steel production serve the nation's growth. Chicago is both a major port and railroad center for the nation.

INDIANA

A quiet and prosperous state, Indiana reaches from Lake Michigan to the Ohio River. La Salle discovered the region in 1679. Soon, trading posts were set up at what is now Fort Wayne, at Lafayette, and Vincennes.

After the British victory in 1763, settlers were forbidden to migrate west of the Appalachians. In spite of this, hunters, traders, and settlers made their way through Kentucky and Tennessee into Indiana.

Again it was Clark who captured Indiana for the new United States. In 1800, Indiana, Illinois, Michigan, Wisconsin, and part of Minnesota became Indiana Territory. Under Chief Tecumseh, the Indians again tried to protect their hunting grounds. But Tecumseh was defeated at the Battle of Tippecanoe. By 1840 nearly all of the tribes had been moved west of the Mississippi.

In 1816, Indiana became a state, with Indianapolis the capital.

The "Hoosiers" have a right to be proud of the wealth in mines, timber, soils, and quarries in their state. Indiana limestone for building is famous throughout the Western World. Farms are rich with corn, grain, cereals, vegetables, fruit, livestock, and dairy products.

A leading product is steel. At the lower tip of Lake Michigan are great steel mills, refineries, and factories. Because of its position on the Lakes, goods can be shipped from Indiana to anywhere in the world.

A pioneer in education, Indiana has twenty-two major universities and colleges.

MICHIGAN

There have never been records of the fierce fur-bearer in the state, but Michigan is still called the Wolverine State. The beaver should hold the place of honor, for it was the fur trade that called the first explorers to Michigan.

Pontiac was the war chief here, but Indian tribes were finally forced to submit to land treaties.

In 1813 additional land was added to Michigan Territory. A boundary dispute with Ohio resulted in a brief clash called the Toledo War. In return for giving up her claims to the southern boundaries, Michigan was given her immensely rich Upper Peninsula.

Timber, fisheries, mines, all added to her early wealth. Crops and dairy products today are worth millions yearly. Because of the warming effect of Lake Michigan, fruit is a major crop. Apples, cherries, peaches, and pears are plentiful.

In addition to rich mineral lands, petroleum, cement, building stone, and tile are present. Her greatest industry is manufacturing, with automobiles the most important product.

Of second importance is the tourist industry. Called the Winter–Water Wonderland, Michigan offers over five million acres of public land for camping, fishing, hiking, skiing, and swimming. Beauty spots abound.

There are more than forty-five universities and colleges in Michigan. The first agricultural college of its kind was founded at East Lansing, now Michigan State University.

MINNESOTA

The name comes from the Sioux, meaning "sky-colored water." And water is a major part of this state. The Red River leads to Hudson's Bay through Lake Winnipeg, the St. Louis flows into Lake Superior, and the mighty Mississippi begins here, flowing down to the Gulf of Mexico. In addition, the glaciers left some ten thousand lakes.

Called the Gopher State, Minnesota has a wide range of temperatures. Summer days may average 70 degrees, but winters can reach 40 degrees or more below zero.

International Bridge, under construction in 1961, now links Michigan and Canada above the locks.

In this land of lakes and forests, the Indian found game, fish, and wild rice in abundance. Sioux country at first, they were driven west by the Ojibwa.

By 1851 treaties had opened the land to homesteaders. In ten years, population jumped from 6,000 to 174,000 people. In 1858, Minnesota became a state.

For many years, northern Minnesota furnished timber for the nation. Cutting and fires finally reduced the great belt of pine and hardwoods. But there are still over nine million acres of timberland, and this area has become a favorite vacationland.

Iron ore, granite, limestone, and gravel are all important to the state. But the greatest wealth lies in the farmland. Corn, grains, potatoes, hay are only a few of the major products. Minnesota is a leading producer of creamery butter.

Duluth is the major transportation center on the Lakes for shipping grain and iron ore.

During the great European migration, many settlers found a new life here. Today most citizens boast ancestors from Germany and the Scandinavian countries.

NEW YORK

As early as 1614, trading posts sprang up on Manhattan Island for the Dutch East Indies Company. The Dutch tried to remain friends with the Indians, and their purchase of Manhattan for about $24 was the greatest bargain of all time. But the Dutch were not to keep their possession for long.

Only five years before, the French led an exploring party down Lake Champlain. Champlain himself offered to lead an attack against the Iroquois. This gesture gained the

French Algonquian allies, but the Iroquois were to remain bitter enemies for generations.

As for the Iroquois, they had united into the powerful confederacy called the Five Nations. Tribes were the Oneidas, Onondagas, Cayugas, Mohawks, and Senecas. In 1715 the Tuscaroras joined, making them the Six Nations.

By 1664, the British had taken New York and held it until 1777 when Burgoyne met final defeat at Saratoga. New York City became the nation's first capital. George Washington was inaugurated there in 1789.

After 1812, Governor De Witt Clinton's "Big Ditch," the Erie Canal, opened up the state to both Atlantic and Great Lakes shipping.

After the Revolution, settlers arrived from England, Germany, Scotland, and Scandinavia. After the Civil War, two great waves of immigrants sailed into New York Harbor. The first migration brought the Irish, Germans, Welsh. In the second came Italians, Welsh, Germans, Russians, Slovaks, Jews, Armenians, Negroes, Greeks, and Yugoslavs. By 1940 one quarter of the population were immigrants representing forty-five countries.

Due in a large part to this rich blend of cultures, New York has become the great marketplace of America. Its population equals about 10 percent of the entire nation. Dry goods, clothing, jewelry, paper, sporting goods, drugs—almost 25 percent of the nation's sales are made in New York. Industries manufacture an even longer list of products, from printing and publications to glass and shoes. Dairying and poultry raising are important also.

Today, Manhattan is a giant on a small island surrounded by boroughs holding other millions of people in our nation's largest city.

OHIO

This land of the Mound Builders was first visited by the French and British traders. The Ohio River provided excellent transportation, and by 1750 a line of French forts had been built to hold back the British.

It was here that young George Washington, under orders, attempted to take the territory for England and failed. But by the end of the war, the area was British, and after the Revolution, American. Part of this rich land was then set aside to pay military expenses as well as the soldiers who had fought for freedom.

A group of veterans under Rufus Putnam traveled west from Massachusetts to the Ohio River. Here they built a boat and sailed to the mouth of the Muskingum. Here, in 1788, they founded the town of Marietta.

By 1789 settlers on flatboats began arriving by the hundreds. Indian trouble followed. Led by Little Turtle, the Miamis defeated the forces of General St. Clair in 1791. But three years later the Battle of Fallen Timbers removed the Indian threat forever.

Now that the country was safe for further settlement, the first major road was cut through, called Zane's Trace. New Englanders began settling in the north, settlers from the Middle Atlantic states in the central section, Southerners in the south. With this great number of people moving into the territory, Ohio became a state in 1803.

The glaciers have been kind to this region, depositing rich soil over most of the state. Corn became an important crop in the western section. To the northeast, in more rolling country, there is dairying and general farming. Other crops are wheat, vegetables, potatoes, oats, soybeans. Hogs, cattle, poultry, beef, and sheep are also important products. As for natural resources, coal was mined early in great quantities. Because of this plentiful fuel, iron ore was brought down from Lake Superior to be smelted on the shores of Lake Erie.

These same lake shores were also visited by the famous John Chapman, "Johnny Appleseed," who started many of the apple orchards. Peaches and grapes grow there as well.

Another natural resource, clay, was used to make tile and pottery, and Ohio became first in the nation in the production of these products. With the coming of the automobile, Akron became the rubber-tire center of the nation.

Today its location on Lake Erie and the Ohio River makes Ohio the gateway to the West.

PENNSYLVANIA

Sought after by the Netherlands, Sweden, and England, the land finally became British under Charles II. In 1681 a land grant was given to William Penn. Called Pennsylvania, from "Penn's Woods," it became a colony of Quakers, serving as a haven for all who were persecuted for religious beliefs.

The colony's first city was named Philadelphia (Brotherly Love), which expressed Penn's ideas of peace and friendship to white and redman alike.

After Penn's death, the familiar pattern of unrest and greed began to take hold. Urged on by the French, angered by dishonest traders, the Indians began raiding the settlements. At the present city of Pittsburgh, Fort Duquesne was captured by the French and Indians. Retaken in 1758, it became the British Fort Pitt.

With the start of the American Revolution, Pennsylvania

found herself in the middle of the conflict. The Declaration of Independence was signed in Philadelphia. And it was from the tower of Independence Hall that the famous Liberty Bell rang out the good news.

After the Battle of Brandywine in 1777, the British were once more in possession of Philadelphia. Failing to drive them out, General Washington was forced to retire to the bitter cold of Valley Forge. Then, in 1778, Washington pushed the British back across New Jersey. Once more the Continental Congress took up residence in Philadelphia.

But Penn's teaching was not forgotten. In 1780 the Pennsylvania Assembly passed a law stating that no child could be born a slave in Pennsylvania—the first abolition law in the United States.

In 1787, the United States Constitution was drafted in Independence Hall and until 1800, Philadelphia remained the nation's capital.

History was written again in Pennsylvania with the Battle of Gettysburg, the turning-point of the Civil War.

Pennsylvania lies almost entirely in the Appalachian Mountains. The northwest corner fronts Lake Erie for about forty miles. A beautiful state, it boasts fine rivers, farms, timberlands, where fish and game abound. Because of its wealth of natural resources and its location, so well suited for transportation, the state is second only to New York in industrial products. In mineral production, it ranks first in the nation. Petroleum is another important resource. The year 1859 saw the first oil well in the world drilled at Titusville.

As for ports, in addition to the lake port on Lake Erie, Pennsylvania has the second largest seaport in North America as well as the nation's largest shipyards.

As a farming state, Pennsylvania ranks high in the growing of corn, hay, oats and in dairying.

The state's population is third in the United States and offers a rich background of nationalities. As Penn intended, Pennsylvania has given work and freedom to people of all nations.

WISCONSIN

This is truly the Land of Lakes. Wisconsin has five hundred miles of lake frontage, 1,439 square miles of inland water surface. Of the thousands of lakes large and small, about four thousand have been mapped. Others are almost untouched by civilization. Her rivers offered a main route from the Great Lakes to the Mississippi in the early days of exploration.

Wisconsin's lakes, streams, and rocky heights are results of the unusual action of the ice age. But in the southwestern part lies a region that for some reason was completely untouched by the glaciers. Called a "driftless area," it is the only one of its kind in the world.

From 1850 to 1910, timber was the state's most important product. During those years more than a billion board feet of pine were cut!

Today, dairy farms enable Wisconsin to furnish half of the nation's cheese. Other crops are peas, cranberries, corn, potatoes, oats, hay, and other grains and cereals. Great Lakes transportation, railways, and modern highways have helped industry to grow and prosper.

Wisconsin became a state in 1848. Early settlers had come in 1822 to work the lead mines. Then from 1850 to 1860, Germans came into the state by the thousands. Today they make up the largest national group. Other nationalities came as well. In 1820 the second largest foreign group were settlers from Poland.

Because of this rich national heritage, Wisconsin still celebrates may folk festivals. National costumes are worn, old songs sung, old customs remembered. Folk tradition is well preserved in Wisconsin, the Land of Lakes.

INDEX

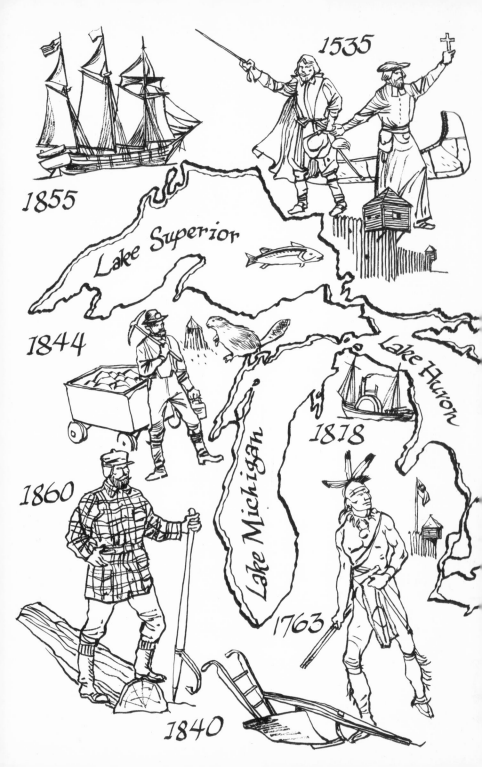

1535

1855

Lake Superior

1844

Lake Huron

1818

1860

Lake Michigan

1763

1840